Come and Believe

Jesus' Words in the Gospel of John and books of James and Peter

Don Pruett

All rights reserved. No portion of this book may be reproduced, stored in a retrieval system, or transmitted in any form or by any means (electronic, mechanical, photocopy, recording, scanning, or other means) without the written consent of the publisher or author prior to usage.

Publisher: Hoot Books Publishing, 851 French Moore Boulevard, Suite 136, Abingdon VA 24211.

Scripture quotations are from the King James Version (KJV) of the Bible for the Gospel of John, Copyright, 1957 by Frank Charles Thompson.

The Amplified Bible (AMP) was used for the scriptures quoted in Peter and James' books. Scripture taken from the Amplified Bible, Copyright 1954, 1958, 1962, 1964, 1965, 1987 by the Lockman Foundation. Used with permission.

Commentaries and Bibles used for research include:
- NIV Zondervan Study Bible (commentary only). Copyright 2015 by Zondervan, Grand Rapids, MI. Any material used from the commentary is within Zondervan's limits that do not require prior written permission.
- Wilmington's Guide to the Bible. Copyright 1981, 1984, 1990, 1991, 2011 by H. L. Wilmington, published by Tyndale House Publishers, Inc., Carol Stream, IL. This text is within Tyndale House Publishers fair-use guideline, and no permission is required.

- Thompson's Chain-Reference Bible, (KJV), Third Improved Edition. Copyright 1934, published by B. B. Kirkbride Bible Co. Inc., Indianapolis, IN.
- The Amplified Bible, published by Zondervan, Grand Rapids, MI. Copyright by The Lockman Foundation, 1987. Library of Congress Control Number: 2013946744.

The song lyrics at the end of most chapters in John's lessons show no current copyrights or publishers. All lyrics used are public domain since they were published prior to 1926.

Some words in *(italics)* were added for clarification purposes.

Copyright © 2022 Don Pruett
ISBN: 979-8-9860608-3-5

Victoria Fletcher
hootbookspublishing.biz
vfletcher56@gmail.com

Dedication

This book was written with my family in mind. God blessed me with Godly parents, a wonderful wife, son, and daughter. We had an ideal family until the enemy death invaded.

Now we eagerly await Jesus' return when He raptures His church and families will be reunited.

Betty Pruett, wife
Barry Pruett, son
Elizabeth "Beth" Gates, daughter
Willie Pruett, father
Eula Pruett, mother

Looking for that blessed hope and the glorious appearing of the great God and our Savior Jesus Christ who gave himself for us that He might redeem us from all iniquity and purify unto Himself a peculiar people, zealous of good works. Titus 2:13-14

Introduction

God sent His only Son, Jesus Christ, from Heaven to Earth for one purpose: to seek and to save the lost. Christ came to the nation of Israel and the Jews first because He was born of Jewish earthly parents. The Jews are God's chosen people.

The Jews were firm believers in the Old Testament Law that was initially given to Moses on Mount Sanai. Jesus came to fulfill that Law and deliver God's message of mercy, grace, and forgiveness. Many Jews accepted the message of Christ, but many others rejected Him. They could not believe Jesus came from heaven since they knew Mary and Joseph were His earthly parents.

After many Jews rejected Jesus, He then offered His message to the Gentiles. He offers salvation in the 21st century to all who will believe regardless of social status, race, or nationality.

"Come and Believe" was inspired by the Apostles John, Peter, and James who recorded many of Jesus' words and deeds. Because of the Jew's disbelief, Jesus used the method of repetition to prove His heavenly origin as the Son of God. Consequently, "Come and Believe" is also repetitious especially in John's Gospel as it echoes the words of Christ.

It is the author's hope and prayer this book will encourage those who have accepted Christ as their Lord to seek a closer walk with Him. To those who have not accepted Christ, our prayer is that you will ask Jesus to come into your heart. This is the best decision you will ever make in this life.

Special thanks are extended to two dear friends who assisted and encouraged the writing of this book: Ralph Sproles, a retired minister and Melody Margrave have made this a much better presentation of Jesus' life on earth and His message to us.

Table of Contents

Dedication..iv
Introduction..v
The Gospel of John..1
Chapter One..**2**
    The Light & the Lamb...2
Chapter Two..**12**
    Jesus' Ministry Launch..12
Chapter Three...**22**
    The Love of God..22
Chapter Four...**32**
    The Woman at the Well..32
Chapter Five..**41**
    Life and Judgment..41
Chapter Six..**52**
    Little is Much...52
Chapter Seven..**62**
    The Bread of Life..62
Chapter Eight..**72**
    Who is He?..72
Chapter Nine...**82**
    The Light of the World, Part 1.......................................82
Chapter Ten...**92**
    The Light of the World, Part Two..................................92
Chapter Eleven...**99**
    The Good Shepherd..99

Come and Believe

Chapter Twelve	**108**
The Power of Christ	108
Chapter Thirteen	**116**
Dead Seed, Bountiful Harvest	116
Chapter Fourteen	**127**
Humility	127
Chapter Fifteen	**134**
The Great Reveal	134
Chapter Sixteen	**142**
One in Christ	142
Chapter Seventeen	**151**
Christ's Gift	151
Chapter Eighteen	**160**
Intercessory Prayers	160
Chapter Nineteen	**169**
Betrayal, Arrest and Denial	169
Chapter Twenty	**180**
Hallelujah for Our Hope	180
Chapter Twenty-one	**191**
The Challenge	191
Introduction to Peter	201
Chapter Twenty-two	**203**
The Sure Foundation	203
Chapter Twenty-three	**213**
The Chosen Stone	213
Chapter Twenty-four	**224**
Submission	224

Chapter Twenty-five	**235**
Serving and Suffering	235
Chapter Twenty-six	**245**
Shepherd of the Flock	245
Chapter Twenty-seven	**255**
The Faithful	255
Chapter Twenty-eight	**264**
Deceptive Teachers	264
Chapter Twenty-nine	**274**
The Promise of God	274
Introduction to James	281
Chapter Thirty	**282**
Gain through Loss	282
Chapter Thirty-one	**295**
Faith and Works	295
Chapter Thirty-two	**306**
The Tongue and Wisdom	306
Chapter Thirty-three	**316**
Pride and Boasting	316
Chapter Thirty-four	**325**
Perseverance	326
About the Author	336

Don Pruett

The Gospel of John

All scripture verses included in these lessons from John were taken from the King James Version (KJV) of the Holy Bible.

Chapter One
The Light & the Lamb

John was called the beloved disciple by Christ; he obviously enjoyed a very special relationship with Jesus. The Gospels of Matthew, Mark, and Luke were written 40-50 years before John wrote his gospel account of the life, death, resurrection and ascension of Christ. John's gospel covers Christ's ministry from His immersion to His ascension back to heaven.

Each gospel writer took a different approach in their account of Jesus. Matthew focused on the fulfillment of Christ's kingdom; Mark concentrated on the urgency of the gospel; Luke wrote of Jesus, the Son of God; and John conveyed the importance of believing on Jesus the Son of God. The focus of Jesus' ministry included:

- Performing numerous miracles through the power of God
- Telling the Jews repeatedly that God, His Father, sent Him from heaven to earth
- Teaching through many parables

John the disciple is not the same person as John the Baptist. John the disciple was the son of Zebedee while John the Baptist's parents were Zacharias and Elizabeth. John the disciple who wrote the gospel of John had some noticeable character traits as recorded by Mark and Luke. They said John was energetic (Mark 3:17), he was intolerant of false teachers (Mark 9:38), and very ambitious (Mark 10:35-37). Luke wrote that John was vindictive when he wanted Jesus to rain down fire on the Samaritans who hated the Jews (Luke 9:54).

We too can be overly zealous, intolerant, and vindictive on our spiritual journey when we act on our own. Most of John's actions were good, especially when he allowed the Holy Spirit to lead and guide.

<u>Jesus' Divinity</u> (John 1:1-5)

John1:1-2 confirmed Jesus Christ's divinity and superiority over man. Jesus is a part of God as He was present with Him from the beginning of time, even before creation. John calls Christ the Word, and the Word was with God, and the Word was God. He is God's Son. God, Christ, and the Holy Spirit make up the Godhead or the Trinity. Each has a different role in God's plan of redemption. God rules over His creation. Christ and the Holy Spirit were there with God when all things were created and today the Holy Spirit dwells in every believer's heart.

Jesus came to Earth as the Son of God. His singular mission was to seek and to save the lost. When Jesus ascended back to God after His resurrection, He sent the Holy Spirit to live and dwell in the hearts of all believers. God, Jesus, and the Holy Spirit all have a special love for every individual regardless of skin color, nationality, or social status. Any person who accepts Christ as their Lord becomes an adopted child of God. We are all equal in God's eyes.

Christ, the Light (John 1:8-12)

John the Baptist came to testify and preach about the coming Christ, the Light of the World. John 1:8 says "He *(John the Baptist)* was not that Light but was sent to bear witness of that Light *(Christ)*."

Isaiah prophesied that God would give Jesus as a Light to the Gentiles (Isaiah 49:6). Centuries before Christ came to earth, God foreordained that Jesus would be a Light to the Gentiles. Christ the True Light would bring salvation to the ends of the earth. There is nothing fake about Him, for He is genuine, steadfast, and the perfect Light to show all people their way out of a dark world of sin. Isaiah said He would illuminate the way for every person.

When Jesus was born in a stable, His own people *(the Jews)* rejected Him as the Messiah. He came with a Jewish bloodline as He was born of the house and lineage of David; but the Jews did not accept Him as the Messiah. Even today the Jews and other world religions refer to Jesus as a good man, a prophet, an excellent teacher, but not the Messiah.

John the Baptist said in John 1:12 that some Jews would accept Him. The prophet Isaiah said in Isaiah 56:5, "Even unto them *(Jews)* will I give in mine house and within my walls a place and a name better than that of sons and daughters: I will give them an everlasting name, that shall not be cut off."

When we accept Christ as our Lord, He gives us a new name and the right to be His adopted child. He has adopted us out of love. We don't owe our spiritual rebirth to any man, but to God, for we are born of God. Christ is our Light to lead us all the way to paradise.

The Word (John 1:14-18)

John called Jesus the Word that became human flesh as He set His tent among men to dwell with them on earth for 33 years. He was like a nomad as He was constantly on the move during His entire ministry. He didn't own a house or have an animal to ride. God always met Jesus' physical needs although he was like a homeless person. He moved about touching and changing lives wherever He went. This book will show how Jesus made friends and enemies easily.

Jesus' disciples and those to whom He ministered were blessed as they were eye witnesses to God's glory working through Him. He had a human body, but God's glory shined though Jesus as He went about doing good deeds. He was full of grace, kindness, and truth.

Thomas Chisholm wrote a song that says in part, "O, to be like Thee; O, to be like Thee; precious Redeemer, pure as Thou art. Come in Thy sweetness, come in Thy kindness; stamp Thine own image deep on my heart." We need to strive to be more like Him and imitate our Lord.

John the Baptist told the people there would be one who would come after him who would be greater. It is out of God's exceedingly abundant grace that we receive His mercy and blessings every day. Jesus is the source of all truth, and we embrace that truth today. Jesus would never tell a lie, even when He was facing the cross. He didn't back down although He was under extreme pressure as the authorities charged Him falsely before He was sentenced to death.

The Old Testament Law was given to Moses, but Jesus came to introduce God's mercy, grace, spiritual blessings, and truth to all who would come to Him through Jesus Christ. He didn't come to do away with the Law, but to fulfill it. No man has ever seen God, but we believe in Him because Jesus declared Him.

<u>John the Baptist's Testimony</u> (John 1:19-28) These verses contain John the Baptist's testimony of Jesus who was yet to come. The priests and Levites asked John the Baptist in John 1:19, "Who art thou?" He told them first in John 1:20 who he was not by saying, "I am not the Christ." He did not intend to mislead them. They asked if he was Elijah or a prophet, and he told them he was not. John the Baptist said in John 1:23, "I am the voice of one crying in the wilderness, make straight the way of the Lord." These words came direct from Isaiah 40:3 written centuries before. John the Baptist was like a town crier who went ahead of an important dignitary who was to come. He told the people to get ready for the Messiah was coming soon.

This opened the way for Jesus who is the most prominent person to ever appear on the world stage. John the Baptist pre-introduced Christ before His arrival.

The priests and Levites asked John the Baptist why he was baptizing if he was not

Christ or a prophet. He told them he baptized with water, but the One who was to come was so much more worthy. John the Baptist did not even feel worthy to loosen the straps on Jesus' sandals. It is natural to feel unworthy when we come in contact with the sinless Son of God.

<u>The Lamb of God</u> (John 1:29-34)
The next day John the Baptist saw Jesus coming, and he told the people in John 1:29, "Behold the Lamb of God, which taketh away the sin of the world." Jesus was much more important than John the Baptist, for He had existed from the very beginning with God. At God's direction, Jesus came from heaven to earth. John the Baptist baptized Jesus in the Jordan River. In John 1:32, John the Baptist saw the Spirit in the form of a dove descend from heaven and it lit on Jesus. Jesus left His example of baptism that we still follow today. A voice from heaven confirmed Jesus as God's Son.

Jesus was revealed to all mankind as God's own Son, so we need to hear what he has to say. John the Baptist believed without any doubt that Jesus is truly the Son of God.

Jesus told him in John 1:33, "Upon whom thou shalt see the Spirit descending, and remaining on him, the same is he which baptizeth with the Holy Ghost." Notice the connection between baptism and receiving the Holy Spirit. John the Baptist was given a special privilege so he could tell the religious leaders who Jesus was. He introduced Jesus to the Jewish people as the Son of the Living God. This is the launching point of Jesus' earthly ministry. It was now time for Jesus to call His twelve disciples who would work with Him in His ministry.

John and two other disciples saw Jesus as He walked. They said in John 1:36, "Behold the Lamb of God!" There was now no doubt who Jesus was. The disciples followed Him. They called Jesus, "Rabbi" which means Master or Teacher. One of the disciples was Andrew, Simon Peter's brother. Andrew went and found Peter and brought him to Jesus. Jesus told Peter in John 1:42, "Thou art Simon, the son of Jona: thou shalt be called Cephas, which is by interpretation, a stone."

The next day Jesus called two more disciples. He went to Galilee and told Philip, "Follow Me." Philip went and got Nathanael and told him they had found the Messiah. Nathanael asked in John 1:46 "Can any good thing come out of Nazareth?" Philip told him to come and see Jesus. Nathanael came and Jesus told him in John 1:47, "Behold an Israelite indeed, in whom is no guile *(deceit/falsehood)*."

Nathanael wanted to know how Jesus knew him and Jesus replied that before Philip called him, He saw him under a fig tree. Then Nathanael proclaimed in John 1:49, "Rabbi, thou art the Son of God; thou art the King of Israel." Jesus told him he would see greater things. When we see Jesus as the Son of God, great things will happen in our lives. Then Jesus told Nathanael in John 1:51, "Verily, verily (*truly*), I say unto you, 'Hereafter ye shall see heaven open, and the angels of God ascending and descending upon the Son of Man.'"

The four disciples who Jesus called up to this point had come in direct contact with the Lamb of God. They were instantly drawn to Him. They didn't question or hesitate to give up their vocations to follow Jesus and work with Him. All believers have also come into direct contact with the Lord. He gives us salvation and the promise of everlasting life.

Jesus comforted His disciples with a promise in John 14:1-4, "Let not your heart be troubled; ye believe in God, believe also in me. In my Father's house are many mansions: if it were not so, I would have told you. I go to prepare a place for you. And if I go and prepare a place for you, I will come again, and receive you unto myself; that where I am, there ye may be also. And

whither I go ye know, and the way ye know." Jesus has left Earth, but He's coming back to rapture His church and take all His children home with Him forever.
Are you ready for His coming?

> **Where the Soul Never Dies**
> William M. Golden, 1914
> To Canaan's land I'm on my way,
> where the soul of man never dies.
> My darkest night will turn to day,
> where the soul of man never dies.
> Dear friends, there'll be no sad farewells,
> there'll be no tear-dimmed eyes.
> Where all is peace and joy and love,
> and the soul of man never dies.

Chapter Two
Jesus' Ministry Launch

It is exciting when something brand new starts for the very first time. When a couple gets married they look forward to happy days ahead. They don't know exactly where life's pathway may lead, but they are convinced that together they can tackle any challenges. Their hopes and dreams are on a foundation of deep love and respect for each other. They anticipate a long, married life together as one.

Later, one or more babies may join the family, and another new beginning is experienced. The family dynamics change immediately upon the arrival of each baby. Too soon the children are ready to start pre-K, and once again the excitement rises to a new level. Mom and Dad want to see how their child will make new friends and how they will adjust to being at school and away from home. The parent's dreams are large as each child starts developing its potential.

Somewhere along the way the family buys or builds a home. This home becomes a safe haven away from the problems of the world for the entire family. The day's problems can be put aside at the dinner table. Children love to tell their parents what happened that day at school. Times are exciting as the children's development begins taking shape.

The family finds excitement on their annual vacation trip to the beach, the mountains, the zoo, or the aquarium. Times are good and none of the family wants to return from the trip to face a hectic life.

Likewise, there are events and activities in the world that affect us. In 1962, NASA launched John Glenn into orbit and space exploration began. The entire nation was excited that we had accomplished this great mission, and John Glenn returned safely to earth. We were all so proud of America's success. The space program continues to expand and thrive.

New and exciting things are also happening daily in the fields of medicine, science, and telecommunications. Your new smart phone or computer is almost out of date the day you buy it since knowledge is advancing so rapidly. It is amazing how we can now call, text, or message to the other side of the globe and our message is received almost immediately.

John 2 records Jesus' earthly ministry launch. The twelve disciples were no doubt excited, but they had no idea how much difference Jesus would make in their lives and the lives of others. This was the most important launch of anything— before or since—and God was behind it all. Jesus came to show religious people, believers, and unbelievers how His mercy and grace supersedes and fulfills the Old Testament Law.

In the Old Testament, man fell to sin in the Garden of Eden and we became victims because of Adam's sin. God sent His only Son from heaven to earth to show us the way from sin to salvation. We are no longer victims of Satan when we accept Christ as our Lord because we have now become victors in Christ. Jesus makes the difference of being hopelessly lost in sin to having an eternal hope of heaven.

<u>Jesus' First Miracle</u> (John 2:1-11)
Jesus, His mother, and the disciples were invited to a wedding in Cana of Galilee. The host ran out of wine at the wedding reception. Jesus' mother told Him about the problem. Six large water pots that could hold 120-180 gallons of water were there for the Jew's necessary ceremonial purification washing. Jesus told the disciples to fill the water pots to the brim, and they obeyed.

He told them to draw some water out and take it to the host who presided over the wedding banquet. The host realized that it was wine of the very best quality. He thought the bridegroom had held back the best wine for the last part of the celebration.

This is when Jesus launched the first of at least 37 recorded miracles He performed through the power that God gave Him during His ministry.

When the wedding guests realized Jesus had turned water into wine, they knew He was more than a mere man. Mary had utmost faith that Jesus could solve the problem even though He apparently had never performed a miracle previously. Her faith was rewarded when Jesus did the humanly impossible.

His miracles were intended to do much more than just solve an immediate need. When Jesus healed the lame or sick, gave sight to the blind, cast out demons from a person under the complete control of Satan, or raised someone from the dead, He did these things to bring attention and glory to God. His miracles showed a heaven-sent supernatural power that no other man possessed. The miracles proved He was the Son of God.

Jesus can still perform miracles in our hearts when we decide to expel Satan from our life and enthrone Christ as our Lord. We arise from the waters of baptism a new person when we mirror His death, burial, and resurrection. We come forth as a new creation just as Jesus did when He came out of the tomb at His resurrection with a new glorified body by the power of God.

<u>Cleansing the Temple</u> (John 2:12-25)

On the third day after the wedding, Jesus did an amazing thing. He entered the temple in Jerusalem on Saturday, the Sabbath Day. It was time for the Passover Feast and many Jews came from distant points to celebrate. He saw merchants and currency money-changers conducting business in the temple. The merchants were selling animals that could be used at the sacrificial altar. The money-changers were converting standard currency issued by the government into temple currency that could be used to pay the temple taxes.

Jesus did not condemn the merchants and the currency exchangers for performing services that made it convenient for folks coming from out-of-town. The problem Jesus had was they had defiled the temple by using it as a place of a for-profit business. They had turned God's holy temple, a place of prayer and worship, into a market place.

There was a lot of noise from all the buyers and sellers. The temple had been turned into a place of commerce, and it was so disrespectful to God. Jesus made a whip out of cords and drove the merchants and money changers from the temple. He turned the currency changer's tables over, and no doubt, coins went everywhere. Jesus showed them what righteous indignation looked like. He was consumed with anger and jealousy over their disregard for the temple of God. They had disgraced God's house. The merchants and currency changers demanded that Jesus tell them what evidence He had that gave Him the authority to do such a thing.

Jesus told them if they destroyed the temple, He would rebuild it in three days. They thought this statement was ludicrous as it had taken 46 years to build the temple. Jesus was not referring to an earthly temple, but His body that would soon be executed. He was predicting His own resurrection three days after His crucifixion.

While Jesus was in Jerusalem during the Passover celebration, many believed in His name and identified with Him. They saw first-hand the signs and wonders He performed. They wanted to follow this man who could do the impossible. Jesus did not commit Himself to this group as He knew how quickly someone can change their mind and turn away (John 2:23-24).

<u>Nicodemus</u> (John 3:1-21)

Nicodemus was a respected Jewish ruler and a member of the Sanhedrin council.

He was proud to be a Pharisee, one of the religious elite. He had seen and heard about the many wonderful things Jesus was doing and he wanted to know more. He came to Jesus at night when his fellow Pharisees would not see him. Nicodemus didn't need the Pharisees' questioning or criticizing him for being with Jesus.

He told Jesus in John 3:2, "Rabbi, we know that thou art a teacher come from God: for no man can do these miracles that thou doest, except God be with him." He recognized Jesus as a teacher by calling Him "Rabbi." He acknowledged God's power at work through Jesus. No one could do what Jesus was doing unless God was with him. Nicodemus came to learn more although he was not ready to openly accept Christ as the Son of God.

Jesus' simple response to Nicodemus in John 3:5-6 was, "Verily, verily *(truly),* I say unto thee, 'Except a man be born again, he cannot see the kingdom of God.'" Jesus told Nicodemus, "Ye must be born again." God was revealed though Jesus and people could readily see how different His message and actions were when compared to the Old Testament Law. Nicodemus was puzzled. He questioned how a grown man can enter the second time into his mother's womb and be born again through a physical birth. Jesus was not talking about a second natural birth, but He was referring to a spiritual re-birth.

We are dead in our sins, but Jesus came to liberate us through a spiritual re-birth. Jesus asked Nicodemus in John 3:12, "If I have told you earthly things, and ye believe not, how shall ye believe if I tell you of heavenly things?" The Pharisees had seen and heard Jesus firsthand, and yet they did not believe. His ministry was transparent for all to see.

Jesus told Nicodemus He came down from heaven and one day soon He would ascend back to God.

This may have created even more doubt in Nicodemus' mind. In John 3:14, He told Nicodemus that Moses lifted up the serpent in the wilderness, so the Son of man would also be lifted up *(on the cross).*

The Pharisees were bound to the Law, but Jesus came to introduce them to freedom from the Law through God's grace and mercy. Jesus said we must be born of water and the *(Holy)* Spirit. Water cleanses bodily filth and the Holy Spirit transforms hearts. The water of baptism and Jesus' blood washes away the filth of sin. At baptism, we receive the gift of the Holy Spirit according to Acts 2:38. Peter told the Jews who participated in Jesus' death, "Repent, and be baptized every one of you in the name of Jesus Christ for the remission of sins, and ye shall receive the gift of the Holy Spirit."

The Holy Spirit now dwells in every baptized believer to transform and bring change into our life. This universal message of salvation is just as critical today as it was in Nicodemus' day. We must be born again spiritually if we want to enter the kingdom of God.

Jesus told Nicodemus we hear the wind but we don't know where it came from or where it went. So it is with everyone who is born of the Spirit. We may not be able to fully explain the work of the Holy Spirit but we feel His presence and we know He is real.

The power of Jesus' blood to cleanse us from all sin cannot be minimized. When we are baptized we follow Jesus' example at the Jordan River. It is critical that every person who desires will believe the message Jesus told Nicodemus.

John 3:16 says, "For God so loved the world, that he gave his only begotten Son, that whosoever believeth in him should not perish, but have everlasting life." Jesus came to earth for one purpose: to seek and to save sinners. He gave every drop of His blood so we can be cleansed from all sin. Jesus was our sacrificial Lamb on the cross.

Into the Heart of Jesus
Oswald J. Smith, 1914
Into the heart of Jesus,
deeper and deeper I go,
seeking to know the reason
why He should love me so,
Why He should stoop to lift me
up from the miry clay.
Saving my soul, making me whole,
though I had wandered away.

Chapter Three
The Love of God

Love is one of the strongest forces in the world. Its power far exceeds anything ever invented by man including rockets, jet airplanes, weapons, or dynamos. The power of God's love for us is indescribable. In turn, our love for others is critical to a healthy spiritual life.

Nations can be at odds or in a war, but finally the desire for peace out-weighs the need for battle. The two sides may not start loving each other, but they are willing to find common ground for a truce. Couples can disagree strongly, but when they simmer down and work jointly to resolve an issue, they can usually find a solution. They still love each other in spite of their disagreement. There is no room in marriage for verbal or physical abuse. If an agreement cannot be reached, the solution may be to agree to disagree and move forward.

God's love exceeds all other love known to man. A mother's love for her child is probably the second most sincere and forceful love. She sits up during the night to tend to a sick child. Her energy is drained, but her love doesn't fade. Love gives us the ability to work through the problems of life. God's love enables and empowers us to love others, even the unlovable. We can love a person but hate their actions at the same time. Trials cause our love to become real and visible. Most problems are temporary but love remains. When problems arise, our love can grow stronger.

You can probably think of a real-life example where love was evident in very difficult circumstances. Disagreements and opinions can test our love, but true love never fails. Problems can attack love and make it erode over time if the problem is not addressed and dealt with head-on. As God's child, we are to promote love if we are to make a difference.

The Apostle Paul wrote an excellent discourse that defines love in 1 Corinthians 13. He said we can speak like an angel and it means nothing if we don't love. We may have amazing knowledge and wealth, but without love it is nothing. Love is patient and without envy; love is devoid of pride and selfishness; love only considers the truth and is steadfast. Paul said one day we will see Jesus face-to-face and the love He clearly showed mankind on the cross at Calvary.

All of man's love combined cannot equal God's love. His love is sacrificial and everlasting. He commands us to love Him with our entire being, and to love our neighbor as our self. God's plan and purpose for each person is based on His love. God's love is unconditional and unlimited for fallen man. His grace and mercy enable us to extend our love to others, just as God loves us.

<u>Conditions of Salvation</u>   (John 3:14-16)

This portion of the scriptures is probably quoted, taught, and preached as much as any other verses in the Bible. We see God's sacrificial love for sinners by offering His only Son as a blood sacrifice for our sins. We cannot understand the depth of God's love and we certainly don't deserve it. He loves us anyway and offers forgiveness when we repent of our sins.

Jesus said the Son of man would be lifted up the same way Moses lifted up the serpent in the wilderness. In Numbers 21, the children of Israel became discouraged. They detested being stranded for decades in the desert heat and cold, so they grumbled and complained to God and Moses. God sent poisonous serpents that bit the Israelites and many of them died. They asked Moses to remove the snakes. God told Moses to make a serpent out of brass and put it on a pole so any person that looked on the serpent would be saved. This was an Old Testament symbol that foretold the coming crucifixion of Christ centuries later on the cross.

Roman soldiers nailed Jesus to the cross and lifted Him up between heaven and earth just as Moses lifted up the brass serpent in the wilderness. Many stood near the cross as they looked up at Jesus while He died. His death was for the healing of the nations and for anyone who will place their faith in Him. He requires repentance for sin so He can forgive. John 3:16 says He died for whoever comes to Him for salvation. This promise gives us hope for a life in eternity with our Lord.

When we come to Christ, we instantly feel the burden of sin that has been lifted. We see our need for a loving Savior to rescue us from the clutches of Satan. New freedom is found in Jesus when through faith we repent, confess Him as the Son of the Living God, and obey His command to be baptized. This is our way out of sin to salvation. He gives us a hope and a peace we have never experienced.

God's plan of salvation is so simple that a child who knows the difference between right and wrong can understand it. Every person has sinned; therefore, we all need salvation. Not one person can claim they are righteous and without sin. Every person stands in need of God's forgiveness. His love is universal to anyone who wants it.

God loves the terrorist, the rapist, and the murderer just as much as He loves any believer. His love is boundless and it knows no limits. His love is infinite and it is immense. 1 Corinthians 6:20 tells us, "For ye are bought with a price: therefore, glorify God in your body, and in your spirit, which are God's." Jesus paid the price for our sins when He died on the cross. This should cause us to rejoice for what He has done on our behalf.

There are many around us who need to know about God's love and forgiveness. It is the duty of every Christian to tell others about this love; otherwise, they may never know about it. Tell them what Christ means to you and point them to Christ.

You never know what that seed may produce in others. You may see an immediate response, or it may take years for the unbeliever to see their need to surrender their life to Christ.

Our outward man, our bodies, are constantly losing energy and power. This process accelerates as we age. Paul said in 2 Corinthians 4:16, "For which cause we faint not; but though our outward man perish, yet the inward man is renewed day by day." As our bodies get weaker, our spirit grows stronger as we study God's Word. New spiritual strength comes from meditating on the Scriptures and learning more about God. How do we experience a renewing of our Spirit? Romans 12:2 gives the answer. "And be not conformed to this world: but be ye transformed by the renewing of your mind, that ye may prove what is that is good, and acceptable, and perfect, will of God." We must be transformed through Christ instead of conforming to Satan's allurements. We deny Satan and accept Christ as our Lord.

Our minds are renewed so we see the good and the acceptable instead of evil. We understand God's perfect will for our life. Our walk with the Lord becomes joyful and meaningful because our minds have been renewed. This renewal is continuous day-by-day. We are re-charged and re-fueled as we commune with God, our Maker.

Benefits of Salvation (John 3:17-18)

A felon is condemned if the jury finds him/her guilty and they must face the judge's sentence to pay for their crime. After the prisoner serves a good portion of their sentence, they may be released early based on good behavior; but they are at the mercy of the parole board.

Every sinner who has not repented is condemned and will be sentenced to a second death unless we let Jesus come into our life.

He can parole us from our sentence of the second death when we repent and are released from the penalty of sin. Jesus frees us from the imprisonment of Satan when He forgives us. He didn't come to condemn, but He came to save us from sin.

We need not live under the burden of sin because Christ came to fix our sin problem. The load of sin is lifted when we become a new person in Christ. When we believe in Him and follow His commands, we are freed. John 3:18 says if we don't believe, we are condemned already.

When we live in sin we love darkness rather than light. Our deeds are evil so we want darkness to conceal what we are doing. Christ came as the Light of the world to reveal our need for Him. He draws us to His love and forgiveness. His light reveals sin and it shines in our lives after we yield our will to Him. It is a choice we make.

It has been said no good thing happens after midnight. Unfortunately today, people have become so hardened and brazen that they have no problem committing crimes in daylight. They will loot, burn, steal and kill without fear or hesitation. They feel no need for darkness to cover their crimes.

When the Light of Christ shines through us, the world can see there is something different in our life. We exude joy, peace, happiness, and contentment the world does not know. The best sermon you can preach is through your daily actions. Others will definitely take notice. It is our challenge to be more like Christ each day.

Lifting Up Christ (John 3:22-36)

John encourages us to exalt Christ in all we do. John the Baptist was baptizing in Aenon near Salim because there was much water there. This is another indication he was immersing, and not sprinkling, as it took much water.

Some of the followers began discussing purification through baptism. The question was about the difference in the baptisms by John the Baptist and the baptism Jesus taught. John the Baptist baptized for repentance, but Jesus came to baptize with the water and the Holy Spirit. John the Baptist said he never claimed to be Christ as he was sent to bear witness of Christ's coming. Man cannot receive anything unless it is given from heaven, as all good and perfect gifts come from God. Baptism is one of God's gifts to us.

The best man in a wedding understands he is not as important as the groom on his wedding day. The best man stays in the background while the groom is in the spot light. The best man must decrease while the groom increases. This is what happens when we turn our lives over to Christ; we want Him to be the lead person as we follow in His footsteps.

John the Baptist was Jesus' friend, but he did not deserve nor did he seek to be in the spotlight. Christ reigns supreme over all men. Jesus had seen and heard all that heaven had to offer. He testified of heavenly things while on Earth, but many did not wish to listen to His testimony. Intelligent people can hear the gospel and walk away in disbelief. Many heard Jesus' message but they chose to reject Him and, unfortunately, many still reject Him today.

Those who choose to accept Christ have sealed their eternity with God. The gospel is true because it came from God. Jesus said in John 14:6, "I am the way, the truth, and the life: no man cometh unto the Father, but by me." Teachers, preachers, and missionaries have all been called to proclaim God's truth around the world. They are empowered by God through the Holy Spirit to be His messenger to a lost generation. What a privilege we have been given to tell others about our loving Lord.

His love reaches down to us today.

> **The Love of God**
> F. M. Lehman, 1917
> "Could we with ink the ocean fill,
> and were the skies of parchment made,
> were every stalk on earth a quill,
> and every man a scribe by trade.
> To write the love of God above
> would drain the ocean dry.
> Nor could the scroll contain the whole,
> though stretched from sky to sky."

Chapter Four
The Woman at the Well

The fourth chapter of John gives an account in Jesus' ministry that is a favorite among many people. The problems today between Israel and Palestine date back to Old Testament times. The King of Assyria planted seeds of conflict in 2 Kings 17:5-6. The Assyrian army invaded Samaria *(now Palestine)* with a three-year siege. The Assyrians ousted the Jews who lived in Samaria and citizens from four enemy countries moved in to occupy it. This was the beginning of the conflict that still exists today between Israel and Palestine.

The new residents of Samaria were not God-fearing people, as they served gods made with human hands. One of the nationalities even offered their children as sacrifices to an idol god of fire. There was a void in their faith, and they knew it. Even though they worshipped idols, some still yearned to have a relationship with God. They thought they could cling to their idols and also worship God, but this will never work.

Our God is a jealous God and He will not allow us to do what the Samaritans tried. We must choose whether we want to chase after the things of the world or have a close walk with our true and living God. He is supreme and He expects our complete allegiance. We can walk with either Satan or Christ; there are no other options.

Some make money their idol god today, but the scriptures say we cannot serve God and mammon *(money)*. Let's be clear: you can have money and also serve God, but the love of money is the root of all evil (1 Timothy 6:10.) We cannot afford to let money be our god and decrease our dependence on God. He expects a full commitment if we are to be His adopted child.

The people of Israel suffer today at the hands of Hamas, an Islamic resistance group from Palestine and other countries in the region. We have seen how ruthless terrorists are. Other continents have the same problems with terrorists and they operate under the names of ISIS, Boca Haran, the Taliban, etc. They claim Allah as their god and their goal is to either convert Christians and Jews to Islam or kill them. We are concerned for there is also considerable gang violence in America. We are not immune from the work of the devil and the evil he creates.

Samaria was located between Galilee to the north and Judea to the south in Jesus' day. The pagans in Samaria were sandwiched between Jews in both directions. The Jews and Samaritans had a mutual hatred for each other. If a Jew was going north or south, they would often try and by-pass Samaria, as it was a land of heathens who worshiped idol gods.

<u>The Woman at the Well</u> (John 4:1-8)

Jesus needed to go from Judea in the south to Galilee in the north. Jesus said He <u>must</u> go through Samaria, so He had no intention of by-passing the heathen territory. The Samaritans were defiled with Gentile blood in the eyes of Jews, but this did not deter Jesus from going there.

Jesus foreknew about a woman in Samaria that He needed to confront with her sins. She lived in shame due to her sinful behavior, so she came to Jacob's well around lunch time to avoid the other women who came to draw water early each day. She was no doubt looked down upon by the other women, so she just avoided them whenever possible. Jacob had dug the well years before to give the residents drinking water for their families and animals.

Jesus and His disciples had been walking for several hours when they arrived at Jacob's well in Samaria. Jesus sent His disciples into town to buy food for lunch while he rested on the wall of the well.

The sinful woman came to draw water; she did not come seeking Jesus as she thought she only needed water for the day. She knew she was living in sin, so she had no need for questioning or criticism from her neighbors about her marital status. She needed Jesus more than she realized because she carried a heavy burden of sin.

John 4:4 says Jesus needed to go through Samaria while other translations say He had to go through Samaria. It was God's plan for Jesus to be at the well at this particular time. Jesus didn't avoid sinners, as He needed to confront sin head-on at every opportunity. His mission was to seek and to save sinners, so in order to carry out His mission, He had to confront sin. He was going to die for all sinners one day, including the Samaritans.

When the woman arrived at the well, Jesus asked her to give Him a drink. The woman asked Him in John 4:9, "How is it that thou, being a Jew, askest drink of me, which am a woman of Samaria? For the Jews have no dealings with the Samaritans." Jesus told the woman if she knew who asked her for a drink, He would have given her living water. Jesus had no means to draw water from the well, so she wondered how He could give her a drink. She asked Jesus, "From whence then hast thou that living water?" She did not realize she was talking with the Son of God who could meet all her spiritual needs, and also forgive her sins. She asked Jesus if He was greater than Jacob who had dug the well many years previously. Jesus was talking about giving her living water that would give her a right relationship with God.

<u>The Inward Well</u> (John 4:15-18)

Jesus told the woman in John 4:13-14, "Whosoever drinketh of this water shall thirst again: but whosoever drinketh of the water that I shall give him shall never thirst." The water from the well could only satisfy thirst temporarily, but Jesus' living water is like a well that springs up from within that brings everlasting life. She asked Jesus to give her His water so she would never need to come to the well again.

Jesus now needed to confront the woman about her sinful life. He told her to go call her husband and come back to the well. The woman told Him she did not have a husband. Jesus told her she had answered well that she had no husband. He said she previously had five husbands, and the man she was living with now was not her husband. He was being brutally honest with the woman; she needed to clean up her life if she wanted the eternal living water Jesus offered.

The only way to deal with a sin problem is to admit our guilt, repent, and seek the Lord's forgiveness. We cannot rationalize or pretend we have not sinned. We must all face our sins and deal with them if we want the living water Christ offers. She first thought Jesus was a prophet. She already acknowledged He was a Jew. The hardest step for any person who needs Christ is not the first physical step; it is admitting our sinful condition so we see our need for Christ. Only then can we step out on faith to receive Christ as our Lord.

Universal Worship (John 4:21-24)
The woman did not know what she worshipped, but the Jews worshipped God, for salvation is of the Jews. Jesus came from the Jewish race as he was from the house and lineage of David, a Jew. Christ is the source of our salvation, and our salvation comes from God through the Jewish blood line.

Jesus told her that God is a Spirit; and we must worship Him in Spirit and in truth. Our place of worship is secondary to our sincere and honest worship of God. The woman was looking forward to the coming Messiah, so Jesus told her in John 4:26, "I that speak unto thee am He."

She left her water pot and went to the city to tell others that she had met Christ. When we encounter Him and make a life change, we want to tell others the good news. He can bring about life changes at every level. Many Samaritans came to the well and heard Him preach over the next couple of days. Many believed in His message even though they were pagans. Jesus said His reception in Samaria was much better than in his home town of Nazareth.

Jesus told His disciples in Acts 1:8 prior to His ascension back to heaven, "But you shall receive power, after that the Holy Ghost is come upon on you; and ye shall be witnesses unto me both in Jerusalem, and in all Judea, and in Samaria, and unto the uttermost part of the earth." The apostles were expected to evangelize their enemies in Samaria just as aggressively as any other place. There are no off-limits for the gospel message.

<u>The Harvest is Ripe</u>   (John 4:27-38)

Jesus' disciples returned to the well from town where they had bought food for lunch. They asked Jesus to eat, for they knew He must be hungry. Jesus told them He had food to eat that they did not know. The disciples thought someone had already brought lunch to Jesus. He told them in John 4:32, "I have meat to eat that ye know not of." Feeding the sinful woman's soul was more important to Christ than physical food. He wanted to do God's will above all else and finish the work God sent Him to do. Jesus went to God often in prayer throughout His ministry so He would know His Father's will.

He told the disciples in John 9:4, "I must work the works of him that sent me, while it is day: the night cometh when no man can work." There was a sense of urgency when it came to doing God's will. He had to work with as many people as possible while He had the opportunity. We need to do likewise as we tell others about Christ.

Jesus knew his days on earth were numbered. We need to feel that same urgency in doing God's work, for we may not have a tomorrow. Christian workers are compared to a reaper in the field. The soil has been tilled and the seed sown. The rains came and the seed sprouted and grew into a bountiful crop. Now harvest time has come and workers are needed to reap and gather. They will bring the harvest into the barns for safe keeping.

The fields of human souls are also ripe and ready for harvest today. Many need to be brought into God's fold for safe keeping. The gospel has been preached and some have responded. Some unbelievers are still waiting to make a decision for Christ. It is up to each of us to present the truth of the gospel to them so they can decide whether to accept or reject Christ. We can show them eternal safety in God.

Each person has a circle of friends that can be our starting point in telling others the good news of Jesus' birth, death, and resurrection. Your friends may be waiting on you to tell them and be invited to Christ. They may want what you already have. Many people have come to know Christ because someone invited them. We have the same opportunity to witness to our friends who are outside of Christ.

The woman at the well went and told others about Christ, and they came and heard Him. The power of this sinner woman's testimony influenced others to believe. They said in John 4:42, "We have heard Him ourselves, and know that this is indeed the Christ, the Savior of the world." The harvest is ready.

Harvest Time
Mary Brown, 1892
Arise! Arise! The Master calls for thee.
Arise! Arise! A faithful reaper be.
Arise! The field is white,
and days are going by.
Awake, Awake, and answer, "Here am I!"

Chapter Five
Life and Judgment

You may have had a life experience that could be called a miracle. You possibly had a serious problem you were unable to solve on your own. We face all sorts of problems: marital, financial, family, sickness, death, and many more. We may seek the very best help, but no one can solve our problem. When we have exhausted all avenues, we turn to God and seek His help. He has promised if we ask according to His will, He will answer our prayer. We need to be asking God for His help while we are asking man for his, rather than wait until we have tried all other means to solve our problem before turning to God.

Jesus does not come to us today in human form to work a miracle, but this in no way means He cannot still work miracles. Some problems are solved in this life and others won't be resolved until we get to our eternal home where all things will be made new. At times, we may be so burdened we don't know how to pray or how to approach the throne of God with our needs. Romans 8:26 says the Holy Spirit can come to our aid in our infirmities, as He can turn our groaning into prayers to God. He is our earthly intercessor while Christ is our heavenly intercessor. We have two thirds of the Godhead (*Christ and the Holy Spirit*) going to God on our behalf.

If we expect God to answer as we have prayed we must be sure our relationship with Him is right. We need to repent of any sin and ask for His forgiveness. This is still not a guarantee that God will give us the exact answer we earnestly seek, but it certainly improves our relationship with Him. A strong Godly relationship helps us deal with whatever answer comes or any remaining problems we must endure. In many cases when someone approached Jesus with a special need, He addressed their sin problem before working a miracle.

In the fifth chapter of John, we see another miracle of healing; how to honor God and His Son; life and judgment; and finally the seven witnesses to Christ's divinity. Jesus is our teacher and we are His student as we study this lesson.

<u>The Miracle of Healing</u>   (John 5:1-8)

Jesus was in Jerusalem on the Sabbath to celebrate a feast. The Jews had six different feasts or festivals they celebrated throughout the year. These were joyous occasions celebrated by the entire church family for the purpose of fellowship and worship. Jesus must have enjoyed these celebrations with other God-fearing people. The six feast celebrations of the Jews were:

- Passover in April, the first month of the Jewish year: celebrated the exodus from slavery in Egypt and deliverance by the death angel
- Pentecost in late June: commemorated the giving of the Law to Moses
- Trumpets in October: celebrated the coming Feast of Tabernacles and the Great Day of Atonement, a day of rest
- Booths on October 17-22: celebrated the harvest when people lived in booths to commemorate their ancestors life in the wilderness for 40 years
- Dedication in December: commemorated the re-consecration of the temple after being polluted and destroyed by the Syrians
- Purim in March: deliverance of the Jews from Haman.

The pool of Bethesda was just inside the Sheep Gate, one of several gates at the temple. There were five porches around the pool where many sick people usually laid. Some were blind, lame, or paralyzed. They would wait on an angel to come and stir up the water in the pool. The first person who stepped into the water when it moved was healed.

A sick man lay there in the crowd when Jesus visited the pool. The man had been sick 38 years and he had been brought to the pool before. Jesus asked him if he wanted to be healed. He told Jesus he had no one to help him into the pool when the waters stirred. Someone else would always step into the pool ahead of him, and they would be healed. In John 5:8 Jesus told the man, "Rise, take up thy bed and walk." Immediately the man was healed without stepping into the water. He obeyed Christ, took up his bed, and walked. Under the Mosaic Law, no man was to do any work on the Sabbath Day. The Jews saw the man carrying his bed and they reminded him it was unlawful for him to carry his bed on the Sabbath. He told them the man who healed him also told him to take up his bed and walk. They asked who said this, but the man did not know who Jesus was. Jesus had faded into the crowd of people so the man could not see Him. Later that day, Jesus saw the man in the temple and told him in John 5:14, "Behold, thou art made whole: sin no more, lest a worse thing come upon you." The man went and told the Jews it was Jesus who made him well.

When Jesus healed anyone, they were healed immediately and completely. It was not a gradual or partial healing that came over time, but it was instant and complete. Jesus knew He had to face the Jews to answer why He had healed on the Sabbath. They planned to persecute Jesus for breaking the Sabbath Law.

Honor to God and His Son (John 5:17-23)

This was a teaching opportunity for Jesus. He would point out some very important things about God and Himself to the Jews who were being very critical. Jesus told the Jews that He and God had been at work jointly. This upset the Jews and they sought even more to kill Him. He not only broke the Sabbath Law, but now He had made Himself equal to God.

This called for the death of Jesus in their eyes. He told the angry Jews in John 5:19, "Verily,

verily (*truly*), I say unto you, 'The Son can do nothing of himself, but what he seeth the Father do: for what things so ever he doeth, these also doeth the Son likewise.'" He could only do what God showed and empowered Him to do.

It was God who gave Jesus the power of miracles. Jesus repeatedly said He did not claim this power on His own. God showed His Son all things and He gave Him power to do even greater works like man had never seen. They would be amazed in future days as Jesus performed many unbelievable miracles. God gives life and He can also raise the dead. God judges no one but He allows Jesus to be our Judge. God will honor His son, just as some of the Jews honored God. We too must honor Jesus if we want to honor God.

<u>Life and Judgment</u> (John 5:24-30)

John 5:24 says if we hear His word and believe in God who sent Him, we will have everlasting life, and will not come into judgment. We pass from death to life when we heed Christ's commands.

Jesus said the hour is coming when the dead will hear His voice, and those who hear will live. We cannot hear when we are physically dead, but we will hear when Christ comes to rapture the church. There will be a loud shout from the archangel and a piercing blare of a trumpet that will awaken the dead. Today those who are dead in sin can also hear His voice if they desire. They who hear and accept Christ as their Lord will live eternally with Him.

Jesus has eternal life within Himself, just like God His Father. God gives His Son the authority to be our Judge, for God has delegated judgment to Christ. He brought Jesus forth from death to new life after His crucifixion. Through God's power, Jesus conquered death and came out of the tomb in victory.

When He was resurrected, He received a new glorified body that will never suffer or die. Jesus told the Jews in John 5.28-29 to not marvel or be surprised; for the hour is coming when all who are in the graves will hear His voice. There will be a resurrection of life for those who have done well, and there will later be another resurrection of condemnation for those who have done evil.

Jesus will execute judgment according to God's plan. The Jews had never heard such a bizarre truth. All believers now have the blessed assurance of eternal life after our earthly death.

<u>Seven Witnesses for Christ</u> (John 5:31-47)
There are seven witnesses to Christ's divinity in the Scriptures. Four of the seven witnesses are mentioned in John 5. The seven witnesses to Christ's divinity are:

- John the Baptist, the forerunner of Christ
- Christ's own works and words
- God the Father who stated Jesus is His beloved Son
- Old Testament that prophesied the coming Messiah
- Jesus' miracles that show His divine power
- The Holy Spirit that came in the form of a dove when Jesus was baptized
- Believers today who are witnesses to His divinity.

Anyone who denies the divine power of Christ brings condemning judgment upon themselves. Jesus said John the Baptist bore witness to the truth. He was like a bright light that preceded Christ to direct attention to the Lord who was to come. Only some of the Jews accepted Christ as the Light of the world. Jesus said there is an even greater witness than John the Baptist. The works Jesus did on earth were a witness that He is the divine Son of God. Jesus' power to perform miracles came directly from God as Jesus made it very clear on several occasions that His power came from God. He was carrying out God's will when He performed a miracle.

The fact that God sent Jesus from heaven to earth testifies that He is the Son of God. God is proud and well pleased with His Son who willingly came from a perfect place in heaven to an imperfect place on earth so we can be saved from our sins. There is no greater witness to the divinity of Christ than God. The Bible also testifies of Jesus' divinity. Repeatedly the scriptures refer to Jesus as God's only Son. The Bible tells us about the future return of our Lord to earth, and this is a witness to His divinity. In John 5:39 Jesus said, "We search the scriptures, for in them we have eternal life." We need to appreciate and read the Bible often so we understand more about God and His will. The scriptures are like a treasure we store in our hearts to use as strength in our times of trial.

Many Jews rejected Christ and His message. When we don't love someone, we naturally reject them, and this is what the Jews did to Jesus. He held the key to eternal life but they turned their backs on Him. Jesus is the One we turn to in repentance seeking forgiveness for our sins.

Men can bestow an honor on us, but what Jesus offers is so much greater than the applause of men. He stands at your heart's door today hoping you will invite Him in to share in His love and fellowship. If you are a Christian, ask Him for a closer walk. If you have not accepted Christ, let Him in to become your Lord today.

Just As I Am
Charlotte Elliott, 1834
Just as I am, without one plea,
but that Thy blood was shed for me.
And that Thou bid'st me come to Thee,
O Lamb of God, I Come! I come!
Just as I am, and waiting not
to rid my soul of one dark blot,
To Thee whose blood can cleanse each spot,
O Lamb of God, I come! I Come!
Just as I am, tho' tossed about
with many a conflict, many a doubt,
Fightings and fears within, without,
O Lamb of God, I come! I come!

Chapter Six
Little is Much

In John 6, a beautiful picture unfolds. This imagery is a real account of just one of Jesus' 37 recorded miracles. This miracle once again shows the power of God working through His Son to do the humanly impossible.

God can take a small amount of talent that we give Him and do phenomenal things through us. The difficult part for us is to release what we have to God so He can bless and multiply it. Our tendency is to hold tight to what we call our own. Everything we claim as ours really belongs to God. He gives us the health and resources to work for earthly gain; we cannot do anything without God's blessings. God causes the organs in our body to function each day. Every breath and heartbeat is a gift from God.

We possess earthly minds that are limited at best, so we cannot possibly think on God's level. When something beyond our imagination and ability occurs, we give Him praise. We are confident it is the will of God that we experience healing or victories that exceed men's normal capabilities.

God has the power of creation, redemption, and eternal life. Nothing God does is within our power, so we thank Him for His grace and mercy. He created and He sustains His creation. The planets do not stray from the orbits God gave them in the beginning. The sun, moon, ocean tides, and winds are all controlled completely by God. Man cannot alter what God has created for He is in control of His creation. He controls the weather and the seasons.

At times, we would like to touch a sick person and heal them. It is not God's will that we try to alter His plan for someone's life. Man cannot escape his appointment with death for it is universal.

Sometimes the best we can do is to encourage those with special needs and lift them up to God in prayer. If a person prays for God's healing, it is up to God to respond as He wills. We would also like to bring peace during war, but this is beyond our ability. Evil men will continue to wage war on earth until God causes all wars to cease for eternity. In the meantime, we must suffer the fall-out from disease and war.

Our generation has witnessed the deterioration of morals around the world. What used to be sin is now accepted as normal; some refer to it as the new normal. Standards have sunk to a low point. We would like to fix the sin problems of abortion, and crime. It is our duty to pray to God for our national needs. If it is God's will, He will answer the way we pray. An answer can come quickly or it may be delayed as He wills.

<u>A Miracle of Food</u> (John 6:5-14)

The sixth chapter of John opens with Jesus on a deserted, grassy mountainside with His disciples. A crowd of thousands came to see Jesus before He arrived. There were 5,000 men plus the women and children. There could have been 15,000 to 20,000 total people in the crowd. In their rush to see Jesus, the people had not taken time to eat. They had seen His miracles of healing the sick and the demon possessed being set free and they wanted to hear and see more from Jesus.

Jesus sat with His disciples as He looked at the thousands of people on the mountainside outside the city. He had compassion on them as they were like sheep without a shepherd. He taught them many things that day.

The hour was getting late and the people still had not eaten. The disciples asked Jesus to send the crowd away so they could go eat.

The disciples had no means to feed such a large crowd. Jesus asked Philip in John 6:5, "Whence shall we buy bread that these may eat?" Jesus had no plans to buy food as He already knew what He would do to prove His divine God-given power. He was ready to meet the people's physical need for food in a very unusual way. He did this to bring glory to God, not Himself. Philip let Jesus know they didn't have enough money to buy food for so many. They could not even meet the minimum needs of the crowd.

Andrew told Jesus there was a lad in the crowd and he had five barley loaves and two small fish. His mother must have packed his lunch so her son would not go hungry. The little boy gave Jesus his lunch so He could perform an unbelievable miracle. Jesus told the disciples to have the people sit down on the grass. Jesus took this little boy's meager lunch and blessed and multiplied it. He gave the bread and fish to the disciples so they could distribute the food to the entire crowd. Everyone ate until they were filled. Jesus told the disciples to gather up the fragments so nothing would be wasted. They gathered 12 baskets of bread that came from the five small loaves.

The people saw this miracle that occurred after Jesus pronounced His blessing on the boy's lunch and they were amazed at His power. They said in John 6:14, "This is of a truth that prophet that should come into the world." Jesus' blessing on the food made the difference.

The good news is that He also blesses us today. His blessings come to the believer and the unbeliever. What little we give to God can easily be multiplied to bless many. The little boy had to place his small lunch in Jesus' hands so it could be multiplied to bless thousands. We too must surrender what we can give so it can be blessed and multiplied. Imagine the good that would come if every believer willingly released their abilities and just some of their possessions to the Lord. Men's souls could be fed and many would come to know Jesus as their Lord.

After the miracle, Jesus perceived the people would take Him by force to make Him a king. He left the mountainside and departed to another mountain so He could be alone. Perhaps He felt physically drained after performing such a powerful miracle, or maybe He just wanted to be alone with God to praise Him for giving Him the power for another miracle.

<u>The Walking Miracle</u> (John 6:15-21)
That evening after Jesus had fed thousands, the disciples went down from the mountainside to the sea. It was dark when they got in their boat to go across the sea. Jesus was on the mountain, so he was not with them.

Some of these men were commercial fishermen. They were very familiar with the sea at night because much of their fishing was done at night. Suddenly a strong wind started blowing. The disciples rowed three or four miles when they saw Jesus walking toward them on the water. As He neared the boat, He could sense their fear. In John 6:20 Jesus said, "It is I; be not afraid." He boarded the boat and immediately they arrived at their destination on the other shore. Have you ever strongly felt the presence of Jesus, and you knew He came into your storm and calmed it? Perhaps all the problems didn't completely go away, but you knew Jesus was there to lead you through the dark night. What a blessing to have a Savior who will never leave or forsake us.

Application of Miracles

We might wonder how we can read the miracles of Jesus and apply them to our life. Just as God empowered Jesus to perform miracles, the Holy Spirit empowers us to do God's work because of our faith in Him. Our mission field may be in our family, with a sick person at home or in a nursing facility, or with the homeless. It doesn't matter to whom we minister, as there are many unfilled needs in our community and beyond. Little is much when God is in it.

Jesus did not mind getting His hands dirty as He served those who were down and out. He touched lepers that other people shunned and He cleansed them so they could rejoin their families. He applied mud to a blind man's eyes so he could go wash and then see. He went into enemy territory to help a sinful woman see her need for forgiveness. Just as the examples He set, Jesus would have us to willingly do the unthinkable to meet people at their point of need.

Mother Teresa devoted her ministry to serving the needs of the poorest of the poor in Calcutta, India. This little lady with a huge faith and a loving heart did God's work in a marvelous way. The slums were her mission field. She didn't have many physical things to give, so she just gave herself to God and He used her to bless many.

A businessman felt led to financially support Mother Teresa's ministry. She took the man into a slum to show him the need. She saw a filthy man with an open festering wound so she cleaned and bandaged the wound. The man told her after they left he would not have done what she just did for a million dollars. Mother Teresa replied, "I wouldn't either." Little is much when God is in it.

An acquaintance committed her ministry to the homeless in her city. Her ministry launched with one loaf of bread and some luncheon meat. She fed the homeless who lived under the bridge one day after losing her job. Her friends got excited about her efforts to feed the homeless so money started coming in to help her do more. God blessed her small beginning of a loaf of bread and some sandwich meat and multiplied it into a much larger ministry. Little is much when God is in it.

God's Providence

The providence of God is amazing. He blesses both the believer and unbeliever. The believer stops to thank God for His blessings. David wrote in Psalms 23:5, "Thou preparest a table before me in the presence of mine enemies: thou anointest my head with oil; my cup runneth over." David was protected by God as he fled King Saul's posse who tried to find and kill him. God fed David and protected him during the time of his deepest need. He later anointed David and eventually made him king of Israel. God's blessings upon David met his daily needs plus much more. Our God is great as He supplies all our needs. God blesses us when we obey and give back to Him. God gives us seven days in a week and He asks us to give one day back to Him. The first day of the week is the Lord's Day and we need to show our appreciation by coming to His house to worship our Creator and Provider. We are commanded not to forget to worship God at His house for two reasons. First, we are to come to worship and praise God for what He does for us. Second, we are to meet with our church family for fellowship and encouragement. New spiritual strength comes from God to His children as we come together as a family to jointly worship and adore Him.

God blesses us with 100% of our income and He expects us to give a tithe back to Him. In the Old Testament Jacob vowed to give God a tenth of all God gave him, so that set the pattern (Genesis 28:22). In the New Testament Paul instructs us in 1 Corinthians 16:2 to give on the first day of the week as we have been prospered (blessed). God doesn't need our money but He expects us to give in faith that He will open the windows of heaven and pour out a blessing we cannot receive (Malachi 3:10). Tithing is a test of our faith in God that He will supply all our needs. Put your trust in Him as you worship and give back to God.

Jesus said in Luke 6:38, "Give, and it shall be given unto you; good measure, pressed down, and shaken together, and running over, shall men give into your bosom. For with the same measure that ye mete withal it shall be measured to you again." Jesus applies logic to our giving. We freely give and He blesses us abundantly. We give and claim His blessings today. God is not going to let us down when we cheerfully give back to Him. Open your hands, your heart and your possessions to Him and be ready to receive His bountiful blessings.

> **I Surrender All**
> Judson W. Van de Venter, 1890
> All to Jesus I surrender,
> all to Him I freely give.
> I will ever love and trust Him,
> in His presence daily live.
> I surrender all. I surrender all.
> All to Thee, my blessed Savior,
> I surrender all.

Chapter Seven
The Bread of Life

Food and liquids are absolute essentials to life. Most Americans eat at least three meals daily. Some meals may be lighter than others, but most of us have plenty to eat. Americans are blessed well beyond our needs. Our nation is the bread basket for other countries. A big part of our nation's export program is centered in agriculture and meat products. We produce more than we can consume and we are so blessed in America. These blessings from God should never be taken for granted for He provides rich soil, sunshine, and rain for the crops to yield abundantly.

The supermarkets offer many different types of certain food items such as bread. You can buy white sandwich bread, sourdough, multi-grain, rye, wheat, pita, rolls, buns, biscuits, etc. Super markets offer multiple brands on other foods. Choices must be made when shopping so we don't over-buy and waste food.

Bread is so important that it is called the staff of life in the Bible. This reiterates the importance of heavenly bread for our spiritual health and survival. Much is said in the Scriptures about food, bread, and water.

Jesus liked seafood as He ate fish often with His disciples. He liked to hang out with fishermen, although He did not appear to be a fisherman. Instead, He made His disciples fishers of men. In Bible times, the Jews ate unleavened bread during their Passover celebrations. Baking soda and yeast are leavens that make bread rise and become lighter. 1 Corinthians 5:6 says a little leaven spreads through the whole loaf. Jesus is the leaven in our spiritual bread as He enriches our lives with abundant blessings.

Bread from Heaven (John 6:26-27)

In the first portion of John 6, we have the account of Jesus' miracle of feeding thousands of people with a little boy's lunch. After this miracle, Jesus went to another mountain so He could be alone. Some of the people who were in the crowd the previous day found Jesus because they wanted to be with Him again. Jesus said they sought Him because of the physical food He gave them. We can be selfish and expect our physical needs to be met instead of seeking a closer walk with God and relying on Him to meet all our needs. All of us have both physical and spiritual needs, and Jesus is the giver of all good things.

We can be blinded to the power of God when we let our physical wants and needs be the guiding force in our thinking. We can easily labor for temporary perishable things in this life instead of things that last for eternity. We are to never let the excesses of this life become more important than our relationship with Christ. Eternal gifts are given to us and they are sealed by God. Jesus, the Bread of Life, gives us salvation and the hope of eternal life. Knowing this gives us spiritual nourishment.

Jesus' followers asked what they could do to fulfill the works of God. He told them in John 6:29, "This is the work of God that ye believe on him whom he hath sent." God sent Jesus from heaven to earth so each of us can believe in Him. Belief is the starting point of our walk with God. Unless we believe in who He is and what He has promised, our spiritual journey will be meaningless. Faith enables us to believe in a God we have never seen.

The people wanted Jesus to show them a sign so they could believe on Him as the Son of God. They reminded Jesus their forefathers were given manna daily as they wandered in the desert 40 years after their release from slavery in Egypt.

Jesus told them that it was not their leader Moses who gave them manna, but it was God who supplied their needs. He told them God sent the Bread of heaven to give them life.

The manna God provided spoiled quickly but God faithfully gave them a fresh supply of manna each day. The Bread of Life (*salvation*) from Jesus never perishes.

Jesus said they must come to Him and believe in Him to have everlasting bread. In John 6:37 He said, "All that the Father giveth me shall come to me; and him that cometh to me I will in no wise cast out." Whosoever will may come to Christ and accept Him as Lord. He does not cast anyone aside including the vilest of all sinners or even hypocrites.

He did not come from heaven to do His own will, but the will of God who sent Him. Whatever God gave Jesus, He would not lose but will rise up at the Last Day. The believers who come from their graves will arise to meet Him in the air. It is God's plan that all believers will have everlasting life with Him.

Rejection (John 6:41-59)

The promise of a bodily resurrection caused the Jews to murmur against Jesus because He said He was the Bread that came down from heaven. They knew Mary and Joseph were Jesus' earthly parents, so they questioned how He came from heaven. They had the same problem Nicodemus had when Jesus told him he must be born again to be saved. The Pharisees did not wish to understand

Jesus when He said He came down from heaven.

We do not understand all the mysteries of God, but through faith we embrace what He tells us. Jesus wanted them to stop murmuring so He told them in John 6:44, "No man can come to me except the Father which hath sent me draw him: and I will raise him up at the last day."

Jesus repeatedly told them the Father sent Him from heaven and how He will raise people up when He raptures His church. He used repetition in His teaching so they hopefully would understand His truth if they would just choose to believe.

Jesus said that whosoever eats of His flesh and drinks of His blood will have eternal life, and He will raise them up at the Last Day. He said their ancestors who ate manna in the desert had all died, but whoever eats the bread He offers will live forever. This made sense to some, but others doubted and turned away.

When a person turns away from Christ, they impose a death sentence upon themselves. Some of the people said what Jesus was teaching was a hard saying and they asked who could understand. Jesus knew His teachings were offensive to some. People today are also offended by the gospel because it points out our sins. We don't like being told we are in the wrong. However, this does not deter the spread of the gospel to those who choose to believe.

Judas Iscariot stood among the disbelievers. Judas planned to betray Jesus very soon. Christ knows who will accept Him and those who will reject or betray Him. It had been prophesied in the Old Testament that Jesus would be betrayed. He foreknew about the upcoming betrayal that would fulfill prophecy.

Many of the eager disciples who came to learn walked away. They had come to have their physical needs met, so when Jesus told them of spiritual things, they turned their backs on Him. They could not accept what he was saying about His origin in Heaven and His prediction of a bodily resurrection.

They were in the presence of the Son of God, but they walked away. They were being given the hope of a bodily resurrection and eternal life, but they walked away. They rejected the Bread of Life and walked with Him no more.

Jesus asked His twelve disciples, "Will ye also go away?" He wanted them to confirm their faith and dedication to Him. In John 6:68-69 Simon Peter asked Jesus, "Lord, to whom shall we go? Thou hast the words of eternal life, and we believe and art sure that thou art the Christ, the Son of the living God." There was no question in the disciple's minds Who Jesus was, for He was then and still is today the Son of God.

He told them that He chose them as His disciples and one of them was a devil, referring to Judas Iscariot. Judas had as much opportunity as any of the other eleven disciples to be a faithful follower; but instead he betrayed Christ for a little money. The thirty pieces of silver did not wipe away the guilt Judas felt after he betrayed Christ, so he went out and committed suicide.

When we use devious means to gain a little of this world's goods, we can expect to pay the consequences sooner or later. We may not be as burdened as Judas, but we will definitely feel the guilt of sin. Judas was used by Satan to carry out this devious and selfish act and he paid a heavy price for his sin. It is hard to imagine that anyone who had spent three years working closely with Jesus could betray Him.

Satan is powerful and deceitful and he will cunningly convince us it is alright to sin if we listen to him. He will even use lies and deceit on the faithful if we allow it. There is so much to gain when we serve Christ loyally. He blesses us each day with an assurance of hope beyond this life. We suffer trials and tribulations now, but one day our hope of eternal life will be realized. All the problems of this world will vanish and all things will be made new. We will live in joy, peace, and harmony forevermore. Jesus suffered abuse and a very painful death so we can have that hope. He was brutalized with a crown of thorns, verbal abuse, and physical abuse before He went to the cross.

He was mocked, spit on, and slapped in the face because they said He made Himself equal to and blasphemed God. He gave His all because of a love for all men that cannot be verbalized. The Son of God was treated like a felon when He went to Calvary, but He was completely innocent.

The thief on the cross next to Him knew Jesus was no criminal. He asked Jesus to remember him when He came into His kingdom. Jesus told the thief in Luke 23:43, "Today shalt thou be with me in paradise." Jesus still had enough life left where He could forgive the man's sins and save him. Jesus never stopped loving, even as He died a death He did not deserve.

The power of Jesus' blood is amazing. It washes our sins away and casts them into the sea of forgetfulness. Our sins are remembered no more when we repent and turn to Christ. We become blameless because of the blood of Jesus Christ. There is power in the blood of the Lamb!

We cannot fully understand the love of God, nor can we explain it. God looks down in pity on His wayward children and He stands ready to forgive and forget our sins. Parents sometimes face the dilemma of having a wayward child and they don't know how to handle the situation. It is a predicament none of us want when a child is being totally disobedient. Perhaps this is the way God looks at us if we stray from Him as He looks on us in pity.

The summation of this lesson is that Christ is the Bread of Life and the power of His blood washes away our sins. Appreciate what you have in Jesus Christ and commit to serve Him regardless of your circumstances. He gave His all as He died on the cross of shame and pain.

I Gave My Life for Thee
Frances R. Havergal, 1858
I gave My life for thee.
My precious blood I shed
that thou might'st ransomed be
and quickened from the dead.
I gave, I gave My life for thee.
What hast thou given for Me?
I suffered much for thee,
more than thy tongue can tell,
of bitterest agony, to rescue thee from hell.
I've borne, I've borne it all for thee.
What hast thou borne for Me?

Chapter Eight
Who is He?

There are many mysteries of God we do not understand and this is according to His plan. He has a heavenly unlimited mind while our minds have earthly boundaries and limits. We rely on our faith to believe everything God says and does, even when we don't understand His plan. Everything God does is for our good even when we don't see why He acts as He does.

Several books were written but were excluded from the 66 published books of the Bible. Early Jewish church fathers such as Polycarp, Augustus, and others pored over all the books and decided which ones were inspired by God. The Bible had to be without controversy so we can accept it as God-breathed. The Bible was meant to teach and inspire, not confuse. God speaks to us today through the Bible and the Holy Spirit.

The Old Testament prophesies many things and the New Testament echoes and fulfills those prophecies. Many New Testament verses are worded exactly as they are recorded in the Old Testament. The Old Testament and New Testament dove-tail together like two pieces of wood that are joined by a master craftsman. This enabled

Jewish and Gentile converts to accept the New Testament as the inspired Word of God. Some of the manuscripts were excluded from the Bible for obvious reasons. For example, the Gospel of Judas was excluded because it contradicted the four Gospel books written by Matthew, Mark, Luke, and John. Judas wrote that Jesus ordered His own betrayal. He also claimed Jesus married Mary Magdalene, a former prostitute, and they had children together.

Other manuscripts were rejected because they were so far off-base with the accepted scriptures. Some books had interesting historical facts but they had glaring errors.

Some unacceptable books said magic should be used in worship; forgiveness comes through alms-giving to the poor; and the living should give offerings for the sins of the dead. These books were rejected by the church fathers for obvious reasons.

Christians around the world accept the Bible as the inerrant and infallible Word of God. It is not ours to question as we accept the Bible through faith believing it is God's way of speaking to us. We might say the Bible is God's love letter to His children and we accept it just as it is written.

Highly educated but disbelieving scholars have set out to disprove the Bible in the past, only to later accept Christ as the Son of God. The more they read, the more they believed in Him. Their initial unbelief turned into believing that Christ is the Son of God. The more we read about God and Christ, the clearer the Truth becomes. Heaven and earth will pass away, but the Word of God will stand forever. The world may change but God's Word will stand for all eternity. His standard is love and forgiveness through His mercy and grace; and that will never change.

<u>A Divine Delay</u> (John 7:1-9)

Jesus was in Galilee because the Jews in Judea wanted to kill Him. He went about doing good deeds and because of this, He created enemies. His enemies disbelieved that God sent Him from heaven and they could not duplicate His miracles, so Jesus had enemies who wanted to kill Him.

Many listened intently but they turned away and walked with Him no more. Some called Him a Nazarene rather than accepting Him as the Son of God. Even today, good things can come from the smallest villages. It's not about our birthplace or the conditions into which we were born, but our willingness to fully surrender to God.

Jesus was accused by some of breaking the Sabbath when He healed a sick man and told him to pick up his bed and walk. He was accused of blaspheming God by making Himself equal to God. He was innocent of all charges but they became His enemies just because they refused to believe in Him. Jesus did not commit a punishable crime when He claimed He came down from heaven.

The Jewish Feast of Tabernacles was about to take place. This feast was also called the Feast of Booths that dated back many years to their ancestor's wilderness journey of 40 years. The Jews lived in booths or huts during this feast to remember what their ancestors endured in the desert. They read from the Torah, the first five books of the Old Testament, during the feast. They also celebrated a bountiful harvest during this time. Their Feast of Tabernacles resembled our Thanksgiving holiday, but it lasted eight days.

Jesus' blood brothers did not believe in His teachings. They wanted Him to go to Jerusalem in Judea during the feast and put on a display of miracles like they were a circus act. Many Jews who hated Jesus would be in Jerusalem. Jesus knew He would be putting Himself in opposition to the Pharisees if He went there at this time. He delayed going to Jerusalem and He told His brothers His time had not yet come.

The world hated Him because they followed Satan instead of Christ. The Pharisees disbelieved because their confidence was in the Old Testament Law. We cannot be a part of the world and follow Jesus at the same time. Jesus would go to Jerusalem in secret later when He felt the time was right.

Jesus' brothers went ahead of Him to the city and the Jews asked where He was. They wanted to find Him for all the wrong reasons. The Jews were confused when they could not find Jesus in the crowd. They made accusations about Him, but those who believed in Christ were silent out of fear. Only His enemies spoke out against Him.

<u>Challenge to Unbelievers</u> (John 7:16-19)
Jesus challenged His enemies by saying the doctrine He taught did not come from Him, but from the Father who sent Him. If they did God's will, they would understand His teachings. If anyone spoke of themselves, they would be seeking self-glorification, so Jesus said the words He spoke came from God. Jesus told them they broke the Law of Moses and yet they wanted to kill Him because he did good deeds.

They called Jesus a demon and asked who He thought wanted to kill Him. He told the Jews they circumcised on the Sabbath, and He asked what grounds they had for accusing

Him of healing a sick man on the Sabbath. Jesus told them to judge with a righteous judgment.

Is This The Christ? (John 7:25-31)

When Jesus finally went to Jerusalem, He started teaching in the temple. Some questioned if this was the man the Jews wanted to kill. Jesus spoke without fear just as if those in charge did not recognize Him as the Son of God. This was their enemy and no one was doing anything to stop Jesus from teaching boldly. The Jews asked if the rulers understood that He was truly the Christ. They knew Jesus was from Nazareth, but they knew when the real Christ came, no one would know where He came from. Jesus' birthplace was a problem for His accusers.

In John 7:28-29, Jesus cried out loudly, "Ye both know me, and ye know whence I am: and I am not come of myself, but He that sent me is true, whom ye know not. But I know Him: for I am from Him, and He hath sent me." Jesus wanted them to know Him for who He was as God's Son. He didn't cower in fear, although He knew they wanted to kill Him. His time to die had not yet come, so no one tried to arrest Him.

Many believed in Him and asked when the real Christ came, would He do more signs than these which Jesus had done? When they asked who He was, Jesus let them know clearly He was the One sent to earth by the Father.

The Pharisees heard the commotion in the temple crowd so they sent officers to arrest Jesus. He told them in John 7:33-34, "Yet a little while am I with you, and then I go unto Him that sent Me. Ye shall seek Me and shall not find Me: and where I am, thither ye cannot come." Jesus knew He was headed for the cross and He would soon return to the Father who sent Him. The Jews thought Jesus planned on going to teach the Gentiles where He would just blend in with the population, and they wouldn't be able to find Him. They did not understand and they completely misread what Jesus was saying about ascending back to the Father in heaven.

<u>The Promise</u> (John 7:37-39)

Jesus stood in the temple on the final day of the feast and in John 7:37-38, He cried out, "If any man thirst, let him come unto me and drink. He that believeth on me, as the scripture hath said, out of his belly shall flow rivers of living water."

His call is universal today to all who will come and accept Him. Romans 10:12 says,

"For there is no difference between the Jew and the Greek: for the same Lord over all is rich unto all that call upon Him." He came for every person who will hear and heed His invitation. He came for the wealthy and the poor; He came for the rich and famous and the homeless person; and He came for all from every nation.

Jesus is our only way to God. The things He spoke were not the wisdom of man. The Holy Spirit teaches us today as we study His Word. The Bible reveals the spiritual truth of God to us through the Holy Spirit. Jesus promises that all who come will have eternal life. Out of the believer's heart will flow living water to others who need to know Him.

<u>Who is He?</u> (John 7:40-44)

Some thought Jesus was a prophet or a teacher while others said He was the Christ. Some argued that the Christ was to come from the seed of David in Bethlehem, not Galilee. This caused confusion and some suggested His arrest. His time still had not come to die, so no one laid a hand on Him.

The Pharisees asked the officers why they did not arrest Jesus as they had been instructed. The officers said no man had ever spoken like Jesus. They knew He was no mere man or teacher as He is the Son of the Living God. They testified of their belief in

Jesus as the Son of God. Instead of arresting Jesus, they believed in Him.

The Jews and the Pharisees had always approached religion under the guidance of the Old Testament Law. Jesus changed the narrative and talked about the living water and the living bread of life. He plainly said He was sent from heaven by the Father. All this was so strange and different from the doctrine of the Jews.

Nicodemus who had come to Jesus previously asked the Jews if their law judged a man before it hears him and knows what he is doing. The Jews said no prophet had arisen out of Galilee. Jesus' hometown of Nazareth was a problem for them. Nazareth was a small village of a few hundred residents. It did not even have a main road going through the hamlet. The righteous Pharisees could not accept the teachings of any man from such a small village that was off the beaten path. How could the Messiah come from such a lowly place?

Their emphasis seemed to be on the Law and a person's social status. Jesus came to break down all human barriers and rules. He came to open the gates to God's mercy and grace so any one who comes in repentance can receive forgiveness for their sins. He didn't come to do away with the Law but He came to fulfill it.

John Newton was the captain of a slave ship in the 1700s. One night he found Jesus and accepted Him as his Lord. He wrote this beautiful hymn that is loved by millions of people yet today.

Amazing Grace
John Newton, 1779

1. Amazing grace, how sweet the sound, that saved a wretch like me; I once was lost, but now I'm found; was blind but now I see.
2. 'Twas grace that taught my heart to fear; and grace my fears relieved. How precious did that grace appear the hour I first believed!
3. Thru many dangers, toils, and snares I have already come. 'Tis grace hath brought me safe thus far, and grace will lead me home.
4. When we've been there ten thousand years, bright shining as the sun, we've no less days to sing God's praise than when we first begun.

Chapter Nine
The Light of the World, Part 1

Jesus frequently referred to Himself as "I Am." He said in John 6:35, "I am the bread of life." Jesus referred to Himself as "I Am" several other times when He stated at various times:
- I Am the Bread of Life (John 6:35)
- I Am the Light of the World (John 8:12)
- I Am the Door of the Sheep (John 10:7)
- I Am the Good Shepherd (John 10:11)
- I Am the Resurrection and the Life (John 11:25)
- I Am the Way, the Truth, and the Life (John 14:6)
- I Am the True Vine (John 15:1)

Christ used these descriptions to tell who He really is. He is God's only begotten Son, and He became the resurrection and the life on the third day after He was nailed to the cross and His lifeless body was laid in a tomb. He is our all-in-all and it is such a privilege to call Him our Lord and Master. Everything is complete in the great "I Am."

In John 8:12, Jesus said, "I Am the Light of the world." When we accept Him as our Lord, His light penetrates to the deepest recesses of our heart. His light dispels the darkness of sin. We are to let His light reflect out to others who do not know Him.

Romans 3:10 declares, "There is none righteous, no, not one." Romans 3:23 tells us, "For all have sinned, and come short of the glory of God." Not one person can deny their sinfulness. Our sin nature is a curse we inherited from Adam and Eve who committed the first sin in the Garden of Eden. In sin our mothers conceived us. Our mother did not sin when she conceived, as she was given the physical ability by God to bear children. We were all born with a sinful nature into a sinful world, with no exceptions. However, we are not stuck in sin with no escape. There is something we can each do to fix the sin problem in our life.

Christ shed His blood on the cross as our sacrificial Lamb so our sins can be washed away. It is through His blood that the filth of sin can be removed to be remembered no more. This cleansing makes us acceptable in the sight of God. We simply need to accept His gift of forgiveness.

The Adulteress (John 8:1-11)

Jesus was on the Mount of Olives where He frequently went to be alone with God and pray. He must have loved the mountains just as we enjoy the beautiful mountains because they represent strength and solitude. We find serenity when we visit any lofty mountain range. Because of this, it seems easier to commune with God while on the mountain. Christ used these times alone with God where He found new energy and power.

The next day, Jesus went to the temple to teach. The Pharisees and scribes brought a woman caught in adultery to Jesus. The Law commanded that she should be stoned, but the religious Pharisees wanted to entrap Jesus and force Him to pass judgment. Would He follow the Law or break the Law and take some other course?

They asked Jesus what should be done to this sinful woman who had broken the Law. On previous occasions they had seen Jesus' compassion. They hoped He would take a stand against the Law and they could accuse

Him of being a law-breaker. The hands of the accusers were not clean, for they could not keep the very restrictive Law by which they judged others. Regardless, they were going to apply the Law to this woman and stone her. Jesus refused to respond to their question. He stooped down and wrote something on the ground with His finger.

He ignored their pressure and judgment. Finally, Jesus stood and said in John 8:7, "He that is without sin among you, let him first cast a stone at her." It is easy to ignore our own sin so we can judge others. The Pharisees and scribes were sinners too and they knew it.

He stooped and wrote on the ground again. These men knew they were guilty sinners; so every one of them left one-by-one and Jesus was left alone with the woman. He stood and asked her where the accusers were and if no man condemned her. She said no man now accused her. In John 8:11, Jesus pronounced, "Neither do I condemn thee: go, and sin no more."

Jesus did not fall into the Pharisee's trap by judging. Instead, He showed them the wrong of judging people when they had sin in their own life. He didn't need to preach a sermon or give the accusers a tongue-lashing to show them they were wrong. Neither do we need a sermon about our sins to feel the burden and guilt of sin. There is only one way we can be relieved of the heavy burden of sin, and that is through Jesus Christ. He told the woman to go and sin no more. This was the answer she needed most. We have the opportunity to show others the way to God to find forgiveness without passing judgment on their past sins.

Jesus said in John 3:17, "For God sent not his Son into the world to condemn the world; but that the world through him might be saved." Jesus stands ready to forgive instead of condemning. He wants every person to come to Him to receive Him as their Lord. Today, He is our Savior, but at the Last Day, He will be our Judge.

Jesus proclaimed in John 8:12, "I am the light of the world: he that followeth me shall not walk in darkness but shall have the light of life." His light is welcomed as it helps us navigate life's pathway according to His will. His light is invaluable; otherwise, we would be walking lost in darkness like a child in the forest at night. A lost person does not know which way to turn to get home.

Paul said in 2 Corinthians 4:6, "For God, who commanded the light to shine out of darkness, hath shined in our hearts, to give the light of the knowledge of the glory of God in the face of Jesus Christ." We learn of the glory of God when we walk in the light of Jesus.

Jesus Defends Himself (John 8:13-20)

The Pharisees said Jesus bore witness of Himself and His witness was not true. Jesus defended Himself as His own witness. He told the Pharisees where He came from and where He was going; but they did not know or want to know anything about His coming or going. How sad when Jesus reveals Himself and man won't accept the truth. Jesus does not force Himself on anyone who refuses to accept Him as their Lord. We have been given the freedom of choice to accept or reject Christ. The Pharisees and many Jews rejected Him while others accepted Him.

The Jews judged Jesus according to the Law, but He judged no one. He said if He were to judge He would not judge alone as He would judge with the Father who sent Him to earth. Jewish Law said if two witnesses testified the same thing, their witness was accepted as truth. Jesus and God acted jointly and met the requirements of their Law. Jesus said He would not judge alone. Their attempt to entrap Jesus failed once again.

The Pharisees asked Jesus where His Father was. They wanted to see God that Jesus claimed as His Father. He told them bluntly they did not know God or Him. If they had known Jesus, they would have also known His Father. They desired to arrest Jesus, but His time had not come to die, so they did not seize Him.

<u>Departure Predicted</u> (John 8:21-36)
Jesus said He was going away and they would look for Him, but where He was going they could not come. He told them plainly they would die in their sins.

Some thought Jesus was going to kill Himself when He said where He was going and they could not come. Jesus told them they were from below but He was from above. They were of this world, but He came from heaven. He told them again if they refused to believe in Him, they would die in their sins. Rather than repent and receive Him, they continued to disbelieve who Jesus was because they had never seen anyone from heaven. Men must accept Jesus through faith as the Son of the living God if we are to be one of His.

Jesus directed their attention to the time when they would soon hang Him on the cross. He said when they nailed Him to the cross, then they would understand who He was. He said in John 8:28, "When ye have lifted up the Son of man (*on the cross*), then shall ye know that I am He, and that I do nothing of myself: but as my Father taught me, I speak these things." He let them know God was with Him and would not leave Him to be alone. Jesus pleased His Father in all He did. Many believed on Him when He spoke these words.

Jesus told the Jews who did believe Him in John 8:32, "And ye shall know the truth, and the truth shall make you free." They would finally be set free from their ignorance of not knowing who He was. They could also be freed from their sins if they would humbly accept Jesus as the Son of God. Freedom from sin is a wonderful thing, for Christ has taken the guilt of our sins upon Himself. Jesus told them in John 8:36, "If the Son therefore shall make you free, ye shall be free indeed."

He would die on a cross of pain and shame. He was not a felon but He would be treated like one. Then they would know who He was. It was God's plan for Jesus to die an awful death so men everywhere will know who He is and will decide to follow Him.

After Jesus was nailed to the cross, the centurion, who commanded 100 soldiers, and the others watched Jesus die. The earth quaked and they feared greatly saying in Matthew 27:54 that He was definitely the Son of God. The death squad had witnessed darkness during the day time when they crucified Him. They heard Him pray to God asking Him to forgive those who crucified Him because they did not know who they were killing or what they were doing. They heard Jesus say to one of the thieves who hung on an adjoining cross that he would be with Him that day in paradise. Those who crucified Him concluded again that He was the Son of God. It was too late to undo the damage and the soldiers and Pharisees had a load of guilt to bear.

<u>Jesus, the Great I AM</u> (John 8:48-59)

In the closing verses of John 8, Jesus discussed the Jews' heritage from Abraham, the father of the Jewish nation. They were rightly proud to be Abraham's descendants but they could not be proud of their association with Satan. The devil deceived many Jews by causing them to disbelieve what Christ said. Jesus' words meant nothing to them as they were dead-set on killing the precious Son of God who always told the truth. They were blinded to the fact that Satan is a liar.

The Jews said they believed in God but not in Jesus. He told them they did not believe in

God because they refused to believe in Him as God's Son. Jesus said He did not come on His own for the Father sent Him. They intentionally chose to disbelieve everything Christ said. Jesus honors His Father, but the Jews dishonored Him. He said if anyone keeps His word they shall never see death.

They asked Him if He was greater than their Father Abraham who was dead. He told them their Father Abraham rejoiced to see Jesus who would come as the Son of God.

He closed by making a very important statement in John 8:58 when He said, "Before Abraham was I AM." Jesus existed long before their Father Abraham was born. He is our all-in-all as our loving Savior today. Are your eyes open to the divine Son of God who came on a rescue mission from Heaven? He came to release us from Satan's grip.

Open My Eyes
Clara H. Scott, 1895
Open my eyes, that I may see
glimpses of truth Thou hast for me.
Place in my hands the wonderful key
that shall unclasp and set me free.
Silently now I wait for Thee,
ready my God, Thy will to see:
Open my eyes, illumine me, Spirit Divine!

Chapter Ten
The Light of the World, Part Two

The conditions in the world in Jesus' day were not good. Rome governed with dominance over Israel, Caesar ruled with an iron fist, and there was pagan idol worship in their land. Israel was plagued with sin and evil. Jewish long-term religious traditions made it difficult for many Jews to embrace the truth Jesus taught. They had difficulty understanding that God the Father had sent His Son Jesus to earth. When we disbelieve the supremacy of God, our lives are going to be a spiritual train wreck. Without God and Christ, we are spiritually bankrupt.

The Roman government overtaxed the citizens of Israel. Some of the Jews forsook their traditional Jewish beliefs and married pagan Gentiles. The Jews had seen a considerable departure from their beliefs and they had a right to be concerned. Some departed to worship idols and others left Judaism to follow Jesus. There had been a sizeable exodus of Jewish believers from Judaism.

The world is still in a mess today. Conditions have worsened with each generation. We too are being overtaxed and it appears there is no relief in sight. War and threats from powerful nations are a grave concern. Our society is plagued with many evils including accelerating crime rates, etc.

Evil is winning over good at the moment, but God will eventually balance the scales. One day Jesus will put Satan in his rightful place and banish him to outer darkness forever; and all our problems with Satan will end for eternity. Jesus changed many lives during His time on Earth even in the face of adversity and rejection. We are eye-witnesses to the battle between good and evil that rages today.

Healing the Blind (John 9:1-10)

Jesus demonstrated His supernatural God-given power to heal once again. The account is of a poor blind beggar. The disciples asked Jesus whose sin caused this man to be blind. Was it his sins or his parent's sins that caused his blindness? Jesus let them know the man was not blind due to sin, but he was blind so people could witness God's power when He would give him sight. Jesus did not address a sin problem with the beggar like He did in some of His other miracles. He just wanted people to see God's power at work when the blind man received his sight. Jesus said as long as He is in the world He is the light of the world. His light turned this beggar's blindness into a blessing that showed people the power of God. Jesus spat on the ground and made clay with His saliva. He applied the moist clay to the man's eyes and told him to go wash the clay off in the pool of Siloam. He obeyed Christ and he could see instantly for the very first time when he washed the clay from his eyes. From a human perspective, we would say there is no way this could happen, but Jesus was not dealing through human strength as God gave Him the power to give vision to this beggar. God's power was at work in every miracle Jesus performed.

The people saw the healed man and questioned if this was actually the blind man they had seen previously. The blind man confirmed he was, so they wanted to know how he received sight.

The man told them how Jesus anointed his eyes with the clay and told him to wash at the pool of Siloam, and now he could see.

We were all born with a sinful nature and were spiritually blind to God's mercy and grace. We grew and learned the difference between right and wrong and we learned what sin is. Unbelievers are spiritually blind to the consequences of serving Satan. When we obey Christ, we receive our spiritual sight for the first time. Jesus makes the difference when we come in contact with Him and obey His commands. He heals all sinful wounds.

<u>The Threat</u> (John 9:18-33)

Some of Jesus' followers brought the man who received his sight to the Pharisees. These elite religious men knew the Law best. They quizzed the healed man on how he received his sight and who gave him sight. The man related how Jesus healed him with the clay. Miraculous things happen in our lives today when we obey Christ. Our eyes open to God's will and we experience His blessings. Human weakness is turned into spiritual strength when we put our trust in Christ.

A division occurred among the Pharisees. Some declared whoever gave this man his sight could not be from God. The man was healed on the Sabbath and God would not break the Law of the Sabbath that forbade any work on that day of the week. Others asked how someone could heal on the Sabbath if the healer was a sinner. The healed man did not know Jesus' name but he thought He was a prophet.

The Pharisees needed a witness on whether the man was ever blind and had actually been healed. They asked his parents if this was their son who was blind and how he could now see. The parents confirmed this was their son who was blind, but they said they did not know who healed him. The parents feared the Jews; for if they said Christ healed their son, they could be put out of the synagogue. They suggested the Pharisees ask their son since he was of age.

The Pharisees told the healed man to give God the glory for his healing because they now knew the man who healed him was a sinner. They wanted him to believe in God but not Jesus. The man did not know whether his healer was a sinner, but he rejoiced that he was blind and now could see.

They continued asking the man who healed him and he got upset with the Pharisees for their persistence. In John 9:30-33, he decided to speak up strongly for God and the man who healed him. He was not ashamed of God or his healer. He did not fear the power of the Jews who could block him from entering the synagogue. The Pharisees were astounded the healed man was born in sins and he had the gall to teach them. They once again easily overlooked their sins. They could not accept Christ and His Divine powers as this was contrary to the Law.

<u>True Vision and Blindness</u> (John 9:35-41)
Now we come to the best part of the account. Jesus met the healed man in the presence of some Pharisees. They now saw that it was Jesus who healed him. Jesus asked the man if he believed in the Son of God. The man asked

Jesus who the Son of God was as he wanted to believe in Him. Jesus told him he had both seen Him and it was the Son of God who was talking with him. The man's spiritual eyes were opened to Jesus, God's Son. He believed on Christ immediately and worshipped Him. Jesus came into the world so all who are spiritually blind can see. The Pharisees asked Jesus if they were blind. They knew the Law but they were blind to Christ. There is a big difference in physical and spiritual sight. We may have perfect eyesight and still be blind to the love and compassion of Christ. We must understand why Jesus came into the world so we can receive Him as our Lord. We can know about God without really knowing Him on a personal level.

Our spiritual blindness is healed when we yield our lives to Him and invite Him into our lives. We understand that we have salvation because of His shed blood. Christ didn't come to this world to make a name for Himself, although He became very popular.

His teachings and His miracles caused many to follow Him. His sole mission was to seek and to save the lost. He came to give every person the opportunity to accept Him. It is only through Christ that we receive forgiveness and are given the hope of eternal life. He was nailed to a cross to die for our sins. He was innocent and we were guilty, but He died in our place. His blood cleanses us from all sin. We become God's adopted child when we come to Christ. This makes us a joint heir with Christ to all God's riches.

Acts 4:12 tells us, "Neither is there salvation in any other: for there is no other name under heaven given among men, whereby we must be saved." We cannot do enough good works to get to heaven. It is impossible to buy a ticket to get into heaven; otherwise only the wealthy would be there. We must come in faith believing that Jesus is the Son of God and He is our only Savior.

Alas! And Did My Savior Bleed?
Isaac Watts, 1707
Alas! And did my Savior bleed
and did my Sovereign die?
Would He devote that sacred head
for such a worm as I?
At the cross, at the cross,
where I first saw the light
and the burden of my heart rolled away.
It was there by faith I received my sight,
and now I am happy all the day!

Chapter Eleven
The Good Shepherd

John declared Jesus as the Lamb of God who takes away the sins of the world. He said in John 1:36, "Behold the Lamb of God," when he saw Christ approaching. Jesus was our sacrificial Lamb when He died on the cross. God has always required a blood sacrifice for the remission of sins. In the Old Testament, animal's blood was used frequently on the sacrificial altar. People offered one sacrifice after another since they needed forgiveness on a continuous basis. This shows the sin nature that mankind inherited from Adam who disobeyed God shortly after creation.

God's plan was to have one supreme and final sacrifice to cover men's sins once and for all. The cross was Jesus' destiny from the beginning of time. It was not Jesus' desire to go to the cross, but He finally yielded to God's will. He died a painful death and His blood washes away our sins. We don't need to offer a blood sacrifice to God today as Jesus' blood has completely paid the price for our sins. No other sacrifice will ever be needed.

After His resurrection from the dead, Jesus performed many miracles for the glory of God. The people who were healed, freed from demons, or raised from the dead received the benefits of God's glory as His work was done in their bodies. The miracles also brought glory to God and showed the power of God working through Jesus proving that He was no ordinary man.

Jesus' miracles were God's evidence that Jesus was His Son who He sent from Heaven. His miracles were evident, but His message to the Jews was strange.

They could not understand how Jesus came from Heaven as their limited thinking caused them to believe His origin stopped with Mary and Joseph His earthly parents. They could not look beyond their human limitations to see the power of God at work. He is truly the Son of God.

The True Shepherd (John 10:1-6)

The focus in John 10 now calls Jesus the True and Good Shepherd. People in Israel understood the importance of a good shepherd. The most trusted shepherds were those who owned the flock. The shepherd would lead his sheep to green pastures and cool waters. He kept up with every sheep to be sure it stayed with the flock. He administered medication to keep them healthy, and he protected them from predators. A hired shepherd would often abandon the flock in the face of danger, but the owner stayed with his sheep to protect them from rustlers or wild animals. Apply this word picture to Jesus as our True Shepherd who protects us day and night. He never sleeps or takes a day off.

Jesus often used a metaphor, or a figure of speech, when He taught. He told the Pharisees if they did not enter into the sheepfold by the door, but climbed up some other way, they were like a thief or robber. They had no trouble believing in God, but they simply could not accept Christ as God's Son. They did not understand the absolute need to go through Jesus to get to God.

Good works or large donations will not get us to God, although He expects our dedication in serving and giving. Going to Sunday school or on mission trips won't lead us to God, although He expects us to do what we can in these areas. We can only come to God through Jesus Christ, His beloved Son.

Several shepherds would share a common sheepfold for their flocks at night. The only ones who entered the door to the sheep pen were the shepherds. The watchman or gate-keeper opened the door for the shepherds. The sheep listen to the shepherd's voice as they know him. He calls each sheep by name and they understand his voice. In the morning, the shepherd led his flock from the sheepfold.

It is reassuring to understand Jesus knows each of us by our name. He speaks to His sheep through the Bible and the Holy Spirit, and we know our True Shepherd's name. We are to listen to His voice as we know He always has our best interest at heart. He will provide our needs of safety and protection when we stay with the flock. If we stray, He welcomes us back into the flock for He is our True and Good Shepherd.

The true believer experiences trials and afflictions in this life. It is God's plan for us to face these problems to strengthen our faith in Him. Life is not always easy, but we rest in the assurance that our Shepherd is always by our side. He won't abandon us in the midst of our storm.

The mighty oak tree must withstand high winds, drought, sleet, snow, and hail to become a stronger tree. We too must go through storms to strengthen our faith in Him.

As the shepherd leads his sheep from the pen, they follow him. Our Shepherd, Jesus, leads us on our spiritual journey the same way as an earthly shepherd. He will not mislead us or fail to meet our needs. Even if we are persecuted because we claim Christ as our Savior, He will be with us to the end of the way. This earthly life is like God's boot camp to prepare us for heaven. He won't remove all the problems but He will give us strength and lead us through them.

We don't follow a strange shepherd like Satan. The devil's voice may be alluring but we do not follow him after committing our life to Jesus. The Pharisees did not understand it when Jesus was called the True Shepherd.

<u>The Good Shepherd</u> (John 10:7-11)
Jesus told the Pharisees He is the door for His sheep. He is our only doorway to God. He is the One who died for our sins, so He is the only way to God. Only Jesus can offer the safety and security of heaven.

False shepherds make promises they cannot keep. Jesus offers freedom from sin and a peace in times of trouble that surpasses man's understanding.

A child of God receives many blessings in this life and will receive many more in the life to come. Jesus our Good Shepherd offers His peace in times of stress and storms. His love is steadfast and it abides with us each day. Through Christ our blessings are abundant and they exceed our expectations.

The good shepherd lays down his life for his sheep. Jesus laid down His life on Calvary's cross as our Good Shepherd. He doesn't desert us when times get tough, but He is there to lead us through the dark valleys of despair. Satan can scatter a flock through His deceit and lies. He can cause people to take sides and argue. Satan is like a predator that will scatter God's flock if we are not good watchmen and gatekeepers. Christ will help us do the right thing in all circumstances if we look to Him as our Good Shepherd. A united church is willing to follow Jesus and strives to do His will.

After Jesus was crucified and died a horrible death that we cannot begin to describe, God brought Him forth from death in victory. Jesus now has power over life and death. Only in Him do we find salvation and a hope of victory over our trials and even death. One day our Good Shepherd will come and rapture His sheep and take us home to be with Him safely in His sheepfold in heaven forever.

<u>The Shepherd Knows His Sheep</u> (John 10:22-30)

Jesus was at the annual Feast of Dedication when the Jews celebrated the reconstruction of the temple each year after the Syrians had ransacked and destroyed it.

Jesus was walking in Solomon's porch at the temple when the Jews surrounded Him and asked how long He would keep them in doubt. They wanted Him to plainly say He was the Christ. Jesus pointed out their problem of unbelief. He told them repeatedly He was the Son of God but they simply would not accept the truth.

Jesus told them the miracles He did in His Father's name should be enough evidence, but they weren't. Sometimes we too have trouble accepting the truth if it does not fit into our mold. Real truth doesn't change because of human opinions or circumstances. Jesus told them they didn't believe because they were not one of His sheep. He said His sheep hear His voice and they follow Him because they know Him. But the Jews elected to not believe in Christ, so they couldn't begin to understand His truth. They thought they knew the truth, but they didn't.

Jesus said He gives His sheep eternal life and they will never perish. We may perish in this life, but we will never die in heaven. Our mortal bodies that die an earthly death will be transformed into immortal glorified bodies. He told the Jews God had given Him the sheep He shepherds. He said His Father was greater and no one could snatch His sheep from Him. What a beautiful picture of how we move from earth to heaven and reap all its benefits including eternal life. We are safe when Jesus our Good Shepherd protects us like a mother hen protects her chicks when storm winds blow.

Jew's Response (John 10:31-39)

The Jews picked up stones so they could kill Him. Jesus told them He had done many good works in His Father's name. He asked them which of these good works called for His death by stoning. They told Jesus they were not going to stone Him for His good works, but because He blasphemed God. They said He was a man but He made Himself God.

Jesus was anointed and appointed by God to come to earth. He was sanctified and set apart for a special mission. Jesus said if they could not believe in Him, then they should believe in the miracles of God. This upset the Jews even more and they were ready to arrest Him, but Jesus escaped. This was not God's chosen time for Him to die.

Jesus went beyond Jordan where John the Baptist baptized previously and many there believed. Jesus had to change locations to continue His ministry. He is our Good Shepherd.

Savior, Like a Shepherd Lead Us
Dorothy A. Thrupp, 1836
Savior, like a shepherd lead us:
much we need Thy tender care.
In Thy pleasant pastures feed us:
for our use Thy folds prepare.
Blessed Jesus, Blessed Jesus,
Thou has bought us, Thine we are.
Blessed Jesus, Blessed Jesus,
Thou hast bought us, Thine we are.

Chapter Twelve
The Power of Christ

Our God is all-powerful for He is the sole source of power. He had the power to create and He has the power to consummate His plan for man. God has power over all created things including the solar system that has performed flawlessly since creation. He controls the four seasons for the entire globe. God gave Jesus the power to perform miracles. His power is amazing and we accept the fact He is in control of everything. Man cannot alter God's plan for nature or mankind.

God demonstrated His power to deal with Lucifer before creation. Isaiah 14:12-17 says Lucifer was an archangel in heaven. An archangel has many other angels who follow him. Lucifer tried to become the most high in heaven but God put a stop to it. Isaiah said Lucifer would be brought down and he was. He was an angel trying to unseat God, the source of all power. He tried to exalt himself but God cast Lucifer and his angels out of heaven and down to earth. Neither Angels nor any other leader has the power to unseat God from His throne.

Lucifer's name was changed to Satan and today he and thousands of his fallen angels roam the Earth seeking whom they can destroy. He is like a hungry beast looking for prey. He was expelled from heaven by God who cannot be overthrown. God showed his power to Satan who ruins lives, separates families, and divides churches.

God gives us the power to resist Satan and his angels, and to flee from this enemy who wants to send our souls to hell. Christ quoted from the book of Deuteronomy to Satan three different times when he tried to tempt Him. Satan wanted Christ to follow him, but Jesus resisted his temptations of lust, greed, and power. Jesus the divine Son of God has more power than Satan and all of his fallen angels put together.

God's power is recorded throughout the Bible. He freed the Israelites from Egypt after 400 plus years in slavery. He parted the Red Sea so they could escape the Egyptian army who wanted them to return to slavery. They marched through the Red Sea on dry ground and then God brought the walls of water together and the Egyptian army drowned.

God elevated Joseph and David to prominent national positions of leadership after they suffered extreme hardships. God changed Saul from a persecutor of Christians to a preacher to make Christians. God is all-powerful over nature and all mankind.

Although time has passed, God is still as powerful as ever because He is from everlasting to everlasting. As His adopted child, we claim His power today. One day God will give Christ the power to come and rapture His church. Graves of all believers will open and their bodies that now sleep in Jesus will come out of the grave and rise to meet Him in the air. There will be victory over death on that day as believers all over the world awaken to the loud shout of the archangel and the blast of the angel's trumpet.

Lazarus' Illness (John 11:1-4)

Jesus was a good friend to Martha, Mary, and their brother Lazarus. The four of them enjoyed a special friendship. In Matthew 26:7, Mary anointed Jesus' feet with expensive ointment and wiped His feet with her hair. Judas criticized Mary because He thought she should have sold the expensive oil and given the money to the poor. Jesus defended her actions and told Judas they would always have the poor, but they would not always have Him in their presence.

Jesus was away from Bethany where Martha, Mary, and Lazarus lived when He got word that Lazarus was very sick. The sisters sent word to Jesus to come quickly as Lazarus needed Him. Jesus intentionally delayed going to Bethany for two days. He wanted God to be glorified and praised when He responded to their plea.

The situation grew worse while He delayed and Lazarus died before Jesus got to Bethany. He told His disciples before leaving for Bethany that Lazarus was dead. He wanted their faith to be increased when He performed His next miracle.

Jesus had demonstrated the power of God earlier when He raised Jairus' twelve-year old daughter from death in Mark 5:22-43. He also raised a grieving widow's only son in Luke 7:11-17. He just spoke and the two young people started breathing again.

<u>The Comforter</u> (John 11:17-27)

Jesus got to Martha and Mary's house and they were naturally grieving over the death of their brother. They told Jesus if He had been there Lazarus would not have died. Many other Jews were there to comfort Martha and Mary. Martha understood the power of God even in death and she told Jesus she knew that what He asked of God He would give it.

Jesus told Martha Lazarus would live again. Martha thought Jesus was talking about Lazarus living again at the Last Day when all dead believers will arise from the sleep of death. In John 11:25-26, Jesus told Martha, "I am the resurrection, and the life: he that believeth in me, though he were dead, yet shall he live. And whosoever liveth and believeth in me shall never die. Believest thou this?" What a powerful promise that our souls will never die if we believe Jesus is the Son of God. This gives great hope to every believer.

Martha believed what Jesus said and she confessed Him as the Christ the Son of God. Mary then came to Jesus and fell at His feet. Jesus saw her tears and He wept with the two sisters. Jesus feels our pain and sorrow when we lose a loved one to death. His compassion flows to us through the Holy Spirit who brings comfort and peace at the worst times. It was now time to turn Martha and Mary's sorrow into joy.

The Miracle (John 11:39-44)

Jesus' time had come to show the power and glory of God. He told the men to remove the stone from the door of the tomb where Lazarus lay. Martha reminded Jesus of the stench of death since Lazarus had been dead for four days. Jesus told the people gathered around the tomb if they would believe, they would see the glory of God. The stone was removed and Jesus thanked God that He had heard Him. The people needed to believe God had sent Jesus to the tomb.

Jesus shouted with a loud voice, "Lazarus, come forth." Lazarus hopped to the door, bound in his burial clothes, and a napkin still bound around his face. Jesus told the people to free Lazarus so he could move. A very powerful miracle had just happened. God's power over death had been witnessed by the mourners. Many Jews believed on Christ, while others went to tell the Pharisees what had happened.

The tattlers knew how the Pharisees had given Jesus so much grief over past miracles and they seemed to want to add fuel to the fire. Tattling on Jesus was more important to them than Lazarus' resurrection. If they were telling the Pharisees about the good thing Jesus had done and giving God praise, this would have been great, but their motive seemed to be to give the Pharisees more reason to pursue and kill Jesus.

The Pharisees and chief priests were in a quandary on what to do about Jesus. He had performed so many miracles that were drawing people away from the Jewish faith. This created uncertainty in the minds of the Pharisees and chief priests. They reasoned if they let Jesus alone, the Romans who ruled Israel would most likely come and take away their leadership positions and their nation.

Caiaphas was the high priest that year. He told the Pharisees he was well aware of what Jesus had been doing.

He felt the best thing would be for Jesus to die so the nation could be spared. They started planning for His death and it would happen sooner rather than later.

Jesus knew the leaders would find and arrest Him so He took His disciples and went to a secluded town called Ephraim in the wilderness. It was the season for the annual Passover Feast in Jerusalem. The authorities looked for Jesus in the crowd who had come to celebrate but they couldn't find Him. An arrest order had been issued for Jesus if He appeared. Jesus' time to die was approaching but He had more work to do. His time to die had not yet come.

Christ is the first fruits of man's earthly death when He arose after He was executed on the cross. This gives us great hope of our own bodily resurrection if we must pass through death's door before He returns!

Hallelujah, We Shall Rise
J. E. Thomas, 1904
In the resurrection morning,
when the trump of God shall sound,
we shall rise, hallelujah, we shall rise!
Then the saints will come rejoicing,
and no tears will e'er be found,
we shall rise, hallelujah, we shall rise!
We shall rise, hallelujah
in that morning we shall rise.
In the resurrection morning,
when death's prison bars are broken,
we shall rise, hallelujah, we shall rise!

Chapter Thirteen
Dead Seed, Bountiful Harvest

The Bible is full of contrasts...day and night, planting and harvesting, life and death, good and evil, blindness and sight, fallen man and perfected man, and the list goes on. Many times our present circumstances are the result of the choices we make. At other times we may feel like victims due to no fault of our own. There are spiritual choices every person can make that lead to a life of peace or a life of turmoil.

We choose to serve Satan or Jesus Christ; we choose peace over stress with the help of the Holy Spirit; hope over despair, etc. Our choices may last a lifetime. When trouble comes we can ask God for strength and direction, and move on, or we can succumb to our problems. A child of God must never give in to their problems because the Holy Spirit is by our side to lift us up so we can live one day at a time.

The Jews in Jesus' day chose to believe or disbelieve in Jesus. They witnessed His miracles and made a choice. Many chose to believe and follow Him while others departed and followed Him no more. Every person is promised forgiveness when we repent of sin. Forgiveness is God's gift of grace and mercy to everyone who accepts Christ.

The Bible promises our souls will never die. Eventually all believers will have an eternal home with the other saints. Jesus Christ has gone to prepare a place for us and He promised He will come back to get us (John 14:3). This home will not be a remake of what we have on this earth, but it will be a brand-new home made by God's hands. All our problems of this life will be no more and we will live forever with our loving Savior. He gave His all so we can have it all.

Our days on Earth may be long with trials hard to bear. Satan tempts us to complain and murmur against God.

Despair and stress are heavy burdens for many. It may seem our prayers hit a low glass ceiling and go nowhere. Just remember when you are your lowest point, God can lift you up above the problems of this life. One day our earthly life will end. We will either pass through death's door or we may be alive when Christ returns. If we are among the living when He comes back, we won't see an earthly death. There will be an entire generation that does not face an earthly death. Regardless, Jesus is coming to make all things new. We are promised a harp and a crown for the good deeds we have done on earth. Our burdens will be gone and we can live in perfect peace and happiness like we have never known. What a day that will be!

<u>The Anointing</u> (John 12:1-8)

Jesus frequently visited in the home of Lazarus and his two sisters Martha and Mary because of the special friendship they shared. Bethany is the place Jesus came previously to raise Lazarus from the dead. One day Jesus was in their home while Martha and Mary prepared a meal for Jesus, Lazarus, and Judas Iscariot. There were perhaps others in attendance, but these are the only men mentioned in John 12.

At some point, Mary took some expensive fragrant oil and anointed Jesus' feet. She then wiped His feet with her hair. The sweet fragrance filled the house. Judas, the treasurer for the disciples asked why the oil was not sold and the money given to the poor. John called Judas a thief and said Judas was not concerned for the poor as he wanted to get his greedy hands on the money. Jesus told Judas to leave Mary alone, as she had kept this oil to anoint Him at His burial. Jesus said again they would always have the poor with them, but they wouldn't always have Him in their presence.

Greed and pride can sometimes override our desire to follow the Lord's command to help our neighbor or to serve the Lord.

Greed and pride are two of the most devastating things that can easily get us off-track spiritually. Satan tempts us to try and draw us away from Christ. He shows us tempting things we can buy if we don't give our money to the Lord. He may even tempt us to do what it takes to get a raise or promotion, no matter who it hurts. Mary kept her very best for her Lord. Judas' criticism did not keep Mary from doing all she could for Jesus.

The Plot (John 12:9-11)

Many Jews knew Jesus was at the home of Lazarus, Martha, and Mary. They came to Bethany to see Lazarus who had been raised from the dead. Word must have spread quickly when Jesus gave new life to Lazarus as resurrections rarely happened. The chief priests and the leaders in the synagogue wanted to kill both Jesus and Lazarus to remove all evidence of His miracle. Many Jews believed in Jesus that day when they saw Lazarus in good health.

The more miracles Jesus performed, the more the Pharisees wanted to kill Him. They could not duplicate His miracles nor could they accept His message that He had been sent from Heaven by His Father. Jesus was a real threat to Judaism and they intended to stop Him at the cross. They saw the cross as the only solution to their problem.

The Entry (John 12:12-19)

These Scriptures are frequently used on Palm Sunday, one week before the annual Easter celebration for all Christians. Jesus was ready to enter the city of Jerusalem like a King. In Jerusalem, He would soon be arrested and crucified. A large crowd always came to Jerusalem for the annual Passover Feast. During Passover, they celebrated the death angel's passing over the Jew's homes to spare their firstborn from dying. The death angel visited all the Egyptian homes and took their firstborn by death. This gave the children of Israel something very special to celebrate.

They never wanted to forget what God did. They owed God for their freedom from slavery and mercy for their ancestors. Today, Jews around the world still celebrate Passover. They include their children in the celebration so they can carry on this important tradition.

A large group of people came out of the city to the Mount of Olives where Jesus was descending on a borrowed colt. As he rode down the mountain, many people laid palm branches and their cloaks in the path of the colt. In John 12:13 and 15 they shouted, "Hosanna: Blessed is the King of Israel that cometh in the name of the Lord." Jesus told the crowd, "Fear not, daughter of Zion; behold, thy King cometh!"

The Pharisees saw how much excitement Jesus caused. In jealousy and fear, they said He had not accomplished anything. They were very concerned that so many believed in Him so they tried to minimize and neutralize His importance. Jesus' disciples did not understand what was happening that day. They didn't fully understand the significance of Jesus' riding into the city until after He was later killed and resurrected. After His burial, Jesus come out of the tomb with a new glorified body instead of His earthly body that had been laid to rest there three days previously. Shortly thereafter, the disciples understood what had happened.

<u>Dead Seed</u> (John 12:20-26)

A seed of grain or a kernel of seed corn has little value. They are dormant and don't contribute anything to the needs of man. The seed is dead because it has lost contact with the source of life.

Archeologists found seed many years ago when they explored the tombs in Egypt. The seed was several centuries old but it had been in a dry and cool place. The local custom in Egypt was to bury seed and other items with the dead in case they got hungry on their afterlife journey.

The seed the explorers discovered was taken to a laboratory for the scientists to study. Some of the seed was planted and it sprouted and grew as if it was fresh. The seed came into contact with the source of life and it flourished. The soil, plant food, and water were all that was needed for the dead seed to find life.

Our lives are like that old seed. Life is dormant and meaningless without Jesus, the source of life. He gives abundant life and tells us to produce much fruit for Him. When we accept Him as Lord our meaningless lives find the source of life. Our journey lasts for a lifetime as we stay connected with Him.

The Jews came to Philip and told him they wanted to see Jesus. He knew His days were numbered when He told the Jews His hour had come to be glorified. God's plan says we must die in order to receive a glorified body, and Jesus would die like any other human. At His resurrection, Jesus exchanged His earthly body for a glorified and perfect body that was fit for Heaven. Glorified bodies will never suffer or die.

At death, our earthly body is planted like a seed. The body is dead and dormant and will remain so until Jesus comes back to rapture His church. The body has lost contact with the source of life. Our bodies must come into contact with Jesus who will give new life. When He comes to get us, our old corrupt and sinful body will be instantly changed to an incorruptible and sinless body. Our mortal earthly body that died will change to an immortal body that will never die. The first Adam's sin brought death but the second Adam, Jesus Christ, brings life everlasting.

Jesus gave the Jews a parable of a grain of wheat. The seed must go into the ground and die alone; but if it dies and is planted, it produces much grain.

He warns us if we love this brief earthly life too much we can easily lose our life in eternity. When our focus is on life eternal, the value of this life diminishes. He urges us to serve and follow Him, for in Jesus is eternal life.

<u>The Prediction</u>   (John 12:27-36)

Jesus would soon die and give His life as a ransom for many. His soul was troubled at the thought of death. He must have had the Pharisees and the many Jews who rejected Him on His mind as He sorrowed over their plight without Him. Jesus asked God to save

Him from this hour of suffering and death. He then asked that His death would glorify God's name.

In John 12:28, a loud voice came from heaven and said, "I have both glorified it and will glorify it again." Some who heard the voice said it sounded like thunder, while others said an angel had spoken. Jesus explained that the voice from heaven came for the people's sake. They had heard God speak with authority. Jesus told them the prince of this world, Satan, would be cast out. Then Jesus uttered those famous words in John 12:32, "And I, if I be lifted up from the earth, will draw all men unto me." Jesus was lifted up on the cross a short while later so all men who choose can be drawn to Him.

Some believed He was the Son of God while others still rejected Him. They asked Jesus why the Son of man must be lifted up. Jesus told them He would be with them as their Light a little while longer. He invited them to walk with Him in the Light so darkness would not come upon them. Unbelievers walk in darkness but in Christ there is no darkness at all. A person walking in darkness does not know where they are going. The good news is we can walk with our Lord in His wonderful light of truth.

Jesus' light shows us the way through a dark world of evil and sin. In Him we find safe passage from this world to the world to come. If the unbelieving could see His light, they would find forgiveness and healing.

Jesus can take a life filled with sin and make something beautiful from it. He can take a life that is like a lump of useless moist clay and mold it into a very useful life. Lives are changed when Jesus touches them. We just need to invite Him in.

Walk in the Light   (John 12:42-50)

Many rulers believed in Jesus, but some of the Pharisees refused to confess Him for fear they would be put out of the synagogue. They loved the acceptance of men more than the blessings of God. It was their choice to reject Christ. They did not realize it, but when they saw Jesus, they also saw God.

He came to Earth as the Light of the world so whoever believes in Him no longer dwells in darkness. He did not judge or condemn the unbelievers as He came to save them. Judgment in the Last Day will be based on what the Bible says, not man's theory or opinion.

Resurrection Scriptures

For as in Adam all die, even so in Christ shall all be made alive. (1 Corinthians 15:22)

In a moment, in the twinkling of an eye, at the last trump: for the trumpet shall sound, and the dead shall be raised incorruptible *(sinless)*, and we shall be changed.
(1 Corinthians 15:52)

But I would not have you to be ignorant, brethren, concerning them which are asleep, that ye sorrow not, even as others which have no hope. For if we believe that Jesus died and rose again, even so them also which sleep in Jesus will God bring with him.
(1 Thessalonians 4:13-14)

Chapter Fourteen
Humility

Believers and unbelievers can practice humility; but humility is a Christian trait that is very becoming to the child of God. One of Jesus' commands to every believer is that we love our neighbor as much as we love self. This is a tall order, but we can serve others if we have humble hearts.

During times of war, people around the world rise up to help in every way possible. Refugees have so many needs including a safe place to live. They are hungry, thirsty, and many have medical needs. They fled their homes and left their possessions for destinations unknown, hoping there will be a charitable and loving family or organization across the border that will help. Many open their homes free of charge to the refugees. May God bless all those who show humble mercy, love, and compassion to the displaced, hurting, and hungry.

Lesson in Humility (John 13:1-17)

Jesus knew it was time for his departure from this world to go back to His Father. Jesus loved every person who had come to faith and believed in Him. The disciples were with Jesus to eat their final Passover meal. Judas Iscariot was in the group and Jesus knew of

Judas' plan to betray Him that evening. God had placed all power in Jesus' hands. He came from God and now He was going to return to God.

Jesus got up from the dining table where they had reclined and eaten their final Passover meal together. He took off His outer garments and wrapped a towel around His waist. Jesus poured water into a basin and knelt to wash and dry each disciple's feet. He was doing more than removing dirt from their feet; He was teaching them a lesson on humble service to their fellow man.

When He got to Simon Peter, he told Jesus in John 13:6-7, "Lord, dost thou wash my feet?" Jesus told Peter, "What I do thou knowest not now; but thou shalt know hereafter." Peter told Jesus He would never wash his feet. Peter did not feel worthy for the Lord to perform such a lowly task for him. In John 13:8-9, Jesus told Peter emphatically, "If I wash thee not, thou hast no part with me." Peter told Him, "Lord, not my feet only, but also my hands and my head!"

Jesus told Peter the one who bathes only needs to wash his feet. Peter was clean but not everyone in the room was clean. Jesus already knew Judas would betray Him that night, so He said they were not all clean. Jesus finished washing their feet and He sat down and asked them, "Know ye what I have done to you? Ye call Me Master and Lord: and ye say well; for so I am." Jesus told them He gave them an example to follow so they could show humble service to others.

He said a servant is not greater than his master; nor is the person who is sent greater than the one who sent him. In God's eyes, every person is of equal importance. Church leaders are not more important than those who come to God's house to just worship. The disciples would be blessed if they followed Jesus' example.

We may wonder if there is a place for foot washing in worship today. From all indications, this would be pleasing to God as He has promised blessings for so doing. Think of the impact of washing someone's feet where there has been a disagreement. Churches that are divided could possibly gain unity if the two sides came together to wash one another's feet. Obedience always brings blessings. There are, of course, other ways we can be of humble service to others for those who do not feel foot-washing appropriate.

His Betrayer (John 13:18-30)

The Scripture was fulfilled when Judas betrayed Jesus. It was an awful thing he did, but Judas' actions fulfilled Old Testament prophecy that Jesus would be betrayed. Jesus indicated the prophecy was further proof He was the Son of God. He said when He was betrayed they could know definitely He was from God.

Jesus said whoever receives and welcomes Him into their heart also receives and welcomes the Father who sent Him. Jesus was very troubled over what Judas would do when he betrayed Him. Judas had worked beside Jesus for three years and now he was ready to turn on Him as if Jesus was his enemy. In the same thinking today, we must be careful that we do not betray Christ. We may have served Him for years, but Satan can get in our mind and tempt us to betray Him just as he did with Judas. Nothing would please Satan more if we betrayed our Lord.

When Jesus announced someone at the dining table would betray Him, the other disciples asked Jesus who it was. He told them it would be the one to whom He would give a morsel of bread after He dipped it in the sop or the liquid. Jesus dipped the bread in the liquid and handed it to Judas. A piece of moist bread convicted Judas of a crime he was willingly going to commit to betray his Lord. He took the piece of bread from Jesus and immediately Satan took control of Judas. Jesus told Judas that whatever he was going to do to get on with it. There was no need to delay the inevitable. Judas went out into the darkness to meet with those who would arrest Jesus later that night.

The New Commandment (John 13:31-35)

After Judas left, Jesus said in John 13:31, "Now is the Son of man glorified, and God is glorified in Him." The prophecy of betrayal was unfolding before their eyes. God and Jesus were both glorified because God's foreordained plan was ready to be fulfilled.

Jesus told the disciples in John 13:33, "Little children, yet a little while I am with you. Ye shall seek me: and as I said unto the Jews, 'Wither I go, ye cannot come; so now I say unto you.'" The disciples were like little children who needed an explanation of what was happening.

Jesus said in John 13:34 He was giving them a new commandment, "That ye love one another; as I have loved you, that ye also love one another." His entire ministry was based on love and Jesus wanted this to be the driving force for each disciple. In the near future, they would go throughout Asia Minor as apostles to teach the gospel message and plant New Testament churches. They needed to go with a deep love for Christ and love for those who would listen to their message of a risen Savior.

Men would know these disciples as Christ-followers because of their love. Loving one another is imperative to being a strong Christian. A church is weakened tremendously when love is not the driving force just as Jesus taught and demonstrated.

Simon Peter asked Jesus where He was going. Jesus told Peter that where He was going, the disciples could not come for now; they would follow Him later when they would meet *(in paradise)*. It would take the death of the disciples for them to be reunited with Jesus. Since all the apostles have died, they have now been reunited with Jesus for eternity, never to part again.

Peter was always full of questions. He asked Jesus why he could not come with Him now. I believe Peter was being truthful with Jesus when he said in John 13:37-38, "I will lay down my life for thy sake." His intentions were good at the moment. Jesus told Peter, "The cock shall not crow till thou hast denied me thrice." Peter carried out Jesus' prediction later that night after He was betrayed and arrested. He denied Christ three times, and then at dawn the rooster crowed. Jesus was betrayed by Judas and denied by Peter the same night.

Where He Leads Me, I Will Follow
E. W. Blandy

I'll go with Him through the garden.
I'll go with Him through the garden.
I'll go with Him through the garden.
I'll go with Him, with Him, all the way.
Where He leads me, I will follow.
Where He leads me, I will follow.
Where He leads me, I will follow.
I'll go with Him, with Him, all the way.

Chapter Fifteen
The Great Reveal

Many things in life are a mystery. Good and bad things happen, and we sometimes wonder why. We may have to say things happened according to God's plan and accept it. When we can't come up with solid reasons for something happening, we have no choice but to accept His will. We don't need to fully understand as we accept His will through faith.

We may have thought a relationship with another person was on solid footing until something happened and the friendship went south. The friendship that fell apart may have occurred over a minor misunderstanding or major disagreement. A strong relationship should be able to withstand a difference of opinion without the friendship disintegrating. The strongest relationships can crumble when Satan drives a wedge.

The words of Jesus were a big mystery to those who elected to disbelieve Him. They heard what He said and they saw His miracles, and yet they disbelieved. We wonder why they could not accept Jesus as the Son of God. Jesus offered Himself as a gift from God to the Jews but they refused to accept His gift. He said and did all He could to reach them. He wanted them to understand His heavenly origin and see God being glorified through His miracles. Many today have the same problem of rejecting Jesus and His message of truth.

<u>The Only Way to God</u> (John 14:1-6)

God's plan of salvation is simple and easy to understand. When we approach salvation with an open mind, it is easy to accept Jesus as our Lord and Savior. We first hear the truth of God's word about our lost condition; through faith we believe in Christ; we confess Jesus as the Son of God; repent of our sins; and are buried with Him in baptism.

These are all steps of faith in accepting the Scriptures without argument. We don't have to study or memorize anything to qualify as a new convert. It is not up to man to alter or short-cut God's plan of salvation.

Jesus tells us to not be troubled. We live in troubling times, but Jesus wants us to put our faith in Him rather than being defined by our circumstances. We may be in a stressful situation or be disinterested in spiritual things because of our circumstances. Our eyes can be opened and we can call on the name of the Lord to help get our spiritual equilibrium. He can fill the voids in our life with peace, assurance, and confidence.

Jesus tells us about a mansion God has prepared for us. Jesus has gone back to God to get ready for our arrival in our eternal home. He promised He will come back to take us to our new heavenly home. He told His disciples they knew where He was going, but Thomas said in John 14:5, "Lord, we know not whither thou goest; and how can we know the way?" Jesus told Thomas in the next verse, "I am the way, the truth, and the life: no man cometh unto the Father, but by me." This clearly maps our way to God. We must come to Jesus to get to God.

The Great Reveal (John 14:7-11)

Some of the Jews had difficulty fully comprehending what He said about His relationship with God, the Father. He clearly stated if we know Him, we also know the Father and if they had seen Him, they had also seen the Father. Philip, one of Jesus' disciples, did not understand so in John 14:8 he said, "Lord, show us the Father, and it is sufficient for us." Jesus repeated what He said earlier that if they had seen Him they had seen the Father. Jesus and God co-exist as one. He made it clear to Philip the words He spoke were not His, as He did not speak on His own authority. It was the Father in Him who provided the works that Jesus did and the words He spoke. Jesus challenged Philip to just believe in God and Him.

It was a mystery to Philip as the disciples had not physically seen God. It was difficult for Philip to understand what Jesus was saying because he could not see God in person. This is when we use our faith to accept what Jesus said. Jesus came in God's image to the Earth to do God's work.

Jesus makes a very important point that when we believe in Him, we should emulate His works of goodness and compassion. Some of His works, such as raising the dead, are impossible for us to duplicate. We have not been empowered to do all the physical things Jesus or even the apostles did, but we can duplicate His love and compassion as we imitate Him in our daily walk.

Jesus then made a comforting promise. If we ask anything in His name, He will do it. This promise needs clarification. If we ask selfishly for a new home, a new car, or a new boat, these items are not just going to show up in our driveway. But if we need a different car to do the work of God or meet our family's basic needs, then He has the power to provide. The secret to answered prayer is that we pray with a pure heart and according to God's will.

Jesus prayed three times before His betrayal and arrest that God would let the cup of suffering on the cross pass from Him. Jesus realized it was God's will for Him to go to the cross. He finally said to God in Luke 22:42, "Not My will, but Thine, be done." When we pray, we seek God's will. Our will must first be yielded to God so His will can be done.

<u>The Gift of the Spirit</u>   (John 14:15-18)

Jesus made two important promises to His children. He promised to come back to Earth and take us to our heavenly home, and He promised if we ask anything in His name, He will answer our prayer.

Jesus had met the people on their level. He touched them in different ways to meet their physical and spiritual needs.

God demonstrated His power through all the miracles Jesus performed. The followers of Jesus had come to depend fully on what He said. It was God's plan to send the Holy Spirit after Jesus ascended back to heaven. The Holy Spirit is with us today to lead, teach, rebuke, convict, comfort, and to meet our spiritual needs. He is with us during times of stress or joy. He brings peace and comfort when we have lost our best friend to the enemy death.

In John 14:16, Jesus promised, "And I will pray the Father, and he shall give you another Comforter *(Helper)*, that he may abide with you forever." The Holy Spirit comes when we obey Christ, and He will stay with us until we breathe our final breath. He is with us today to help us over all the rough spots in life.

John 6:63 says, "It is the Spirit that quickeneth *(makes alive)*; the flesh profiteth nothing (*is of no benefit*): the words that I speak unto you, they are spirit, and they are life." The Holy Spirit makes us alive in Jesus. We profit nothing spiritually in the flesh for the flesh has a sinful nature. Outside of Jesus, we cannot gain eternal life. The Holy Spirit is a gift from God.

The Holy Spirit guides us into all truth. He will not speak of himself, but He will show us things to come. The Holy Spirit glorifies God as He is a conduit of God's love and grace to us. He does God's work through and in us. We don't see the Holy Spirit but we feel His presence and see His works. We are not orphans, but we are God's adopted child and His treasure.

Jesus told the disciples He would soon be leaving them and they would see Him no more. He said in John 14:19, "Because I live, ye shall live also." These words bring comfort to every believer. Jesus also promised if we love Him, He will love us.

Our love relationship with Jesus cannot be replaced by anyone on Earth. Our eternal abode is conditional upon our accepting and following Him to the end. He has done His part on the cross, and now we must do our part to follow Him.

<u>Peace</u> (John 14:27)

John 14:27 is an excellent way to conclude this lesson from Jesus. He said, "Peace I leave with you, My peace I give unto you: not as the world giveth, give I unto you. Let not your heart be troubled, neither let it be afraid." We need not be troubled or fearful when we know the peace that only comes from Jesus. We can bring our troubles and cares to Him and He will give us peace. 1 Peter 5:7 tells us, "Casting all your care upon Him; for He careth for you." Satan brings fear through trouble and trials; but Jesus says, "Don't be afraid." Friends may disappoint and desert us but Jesus says, "Don't be afraid." No matter what negative thing we may be dealing with, Jesus says, "Don't be afraid." We trust Him to the uttermost when we cannot trust our problems to anyone else. We claim all His promises as our own.

Is everything well with you? If not, turn to Jesus who is your forgiver and your burden-bearer. Learn to lay your problems at Jesus' feet and the Holy Spirit will bring peace and contentment.

> **It is Well with My Soul**
> Horatio Gates Spafford, 1853
> "My sin, oh the bliss of this glorious thought,
> my sin, not in part, but the whole,
> is nailed to the cross, and I bear it no more.
> Praise the Lord, praise the Lord,
> it is well with my soul."

Chapter Sixteen
One in Christ

Many years ago we frequently heard a "schoolyard rhyme" about an engaged couple that said, "First comes love, then comes marriage, then comes baby in a baby carriage." This is the ideal dream of what a marriage should be when a man and woman come together as one. In our liberal society today, some couples enter into what is called a committed relationship instead of marriage. They decide to live together for convenience and fun before getting married. They rationalize and say they want to be sure the relationship is going to last before making a lifetime commitment. They need to have their education, careers, income, and health insurance in place before getting married. This is a distorted and selfish human plan, but it is not God's plan.

A man and woman who are truly in love don't need to have every detail nailed down before making a marital commitment. It is good to have a plan in place on the important issues before marriage because this can prevent uncomfortable conversations later. A couple who has love and respect for each other will work together to solve issues peacefully. They come together as one and this is God's plan for their lives. There is no room in marriage for egotism, abuse, or selfishness. Mutual love binds the man and woman together as one. When all things are right in a relationship, then there is peace and cooperation.

When we accept Christ, we become united with Him. God adopts us as His child and we become His treasure. We strive to work in unity with the Holy Spirit to make our marriage with Christ work, for the church is the bride of Christ.

<u>One in Christ</u> (John 15:1-8)

Jesus teaches the parable about the vine and branches. A parable is an earthly story with a heavenly meaning and Jesus' parables are easily understood. He takes something we understand and applies a spiritual meaning.

The parable of the vine and branches is very simple. Jesus is the vine, God is the Pruner, and we are the branches. Many people owned or worked in vineyards in Jesus' day, so they understood and related to His grapevine lesson. God is in control of the vineyard and He will remove unproductive branches and burn them. He will then prune the good branches so they will bear more fruit. It is God's desire that we are productive and bear much fruit. Jesus warns us that if we are not productive, then God has no place for us.

God said He chastens (*corrects*) those whom He loves (*Revelation 3:19)*. This truth applied in Jesus' day and it still is God's method of pruning and correcting us today. God disciplines His children the same as a parent corrects their offspring. Discipline is for our benefit as it keeps us on the pathway to God and helps us behave like one of God's children.

Because of their parent's teaching and discipline, children learn respect for others, honesty, and the value of hard work. It is the parent's job to also teach their children the ways of God. A loving parent hopes this will help their child choose the right friends and stay on the right path.

God will reward the faithful and destroy the unfaithful on the Last Day. His sheep *(the faithful)* will be separated from the goats *(unfaithful).* Matthew 25:21 tells us Jesus will say to the believers when He comes, "Well done, thou good and faithful servant: thou hast been faithful over a few things, I will make thee ruler over many things: enter thou in to the joy of thy Lord."

Jesus said in Matthew 25:30, "Cast ye the unprofitable servant into outer darkness; there shall be weeping and gnashing *(grinding)* of teeth." Jesus tells us clearly to bear fruits worthy of repentance. The ax is laid to the root of the trees, and every tree that does not bear good fruit is cut down and thrown into the fire. Our challenge is to bear much good fruit for the Lord. These scriptures give us God's plan for rewarding the faithful believer and punishing the unbeliever.

Faithful and fruit-bearing believers will constantly stay connected to the Vine who is Jesus. We cannot bear good fruit for Christ without being connected to Him. We can accomplish nothing of eternal value outside of Jesus Christ. If we abide in Him, we can ask what we will and it will be done. We bring glory to God when we bear fruit for Him.

<u>Perfect Love and Joy</u> (John 15.9-17)

Jesus said the love of the Father was in Him, and His love is in us. We must abide daily in His love. This brings untold blessings when we abide and stay connected with Jesus. When we abide in Christ, He gives us His joy. Jesus' command is that we love one another. This is not a suggestion or guideline, but it is a direct command. Jesus' love was so genuine that He laid down His life for us. His shed blood paid the total debt for our sins. He was willing to be our sacrificial Lamb on the cross.

We are to follow His example of love when we deal with our fellow man. If we are Jesus' friend, we will do what He says. Obedience is the true test of our love for Christ. We are His friend and not His servant. Friends have mutual goals and desires. Our challenge is to know the will of the Father so we can be His friend and do His will.

Jesus said we did not choose Him, but He has chosen us to be His friend. We have been appointed by Christ to be His fruit bearers in the world. This is real friendship and bearing fruit is the direct result of our love for Him.

Hatred (John 15:18-25)

Jesus now changes the subject from love to hatred. Many in His day hated Him, so He knew hatred firsthand. They hated it when He said the Father sent Him from heaven, and they hated Him for performing miracles they could not duplicate. His popularity was spreading like wildfire through the nation of Israel. The Pharisees and chief priest were concerned the Roman government would take the nation away from them if they did not find a way to stop Jesus in His ministry. They hated Christ enough to bring false charges against Him so they could crucify

Him. His innocence made no difference to His enemies.

Hatred is a strong dislike for another person. It creates bitterness and division and it destroys relationships. A hateful person is a dangerous person. The Jew's hatred and our sins nailed Jesus to the cross.

Perhaps you have been the target of hate because you took a stand for Christ. You were doing the right thing but this caused others to hate you. Hatred and love are polar opposites. Jesus would have us to be loving people, even if another person hates our actions or commitment to Christ. Jesus loves even the ones who hate Him as He came to die for all sinners.

In Acts 5, the Apostles were preaching, healing the sick, and casting out demons from people who were under the total control of Satan. The chief priest had the apostles arrested and put in prison. He told them to stop preaching. That night an angel freed them from prison without opening the cell doors where the guards were posted. In spite of the warning to not teach any more, they went back to the temple the next morning and resumed teaching. They were arrested again, beaten, and freed with a command to do no more preaching or healing. The apostles left the council rejoicing that they had been counted worthy to suffer shame for Jesus' sake. They were hated because of the message they preached about Christ.

Hatred and fear cannot stop the spread of the gospel. The more the authorities tried to suppress the good news of the gospel, the faster it spread. We are not to be afraid as we know suffering for His sake is a part of being in the army of Jesus. Suffering comes from hatred but overcoming persecution and hatred is the duty of every believer. We should always take the high road when we encounter those who disagree or show hatred.

Jesus said if His enemies persecuted Him, they will also persecute us. They didn't know God or Christ, so they persecuted Jesus for His message and His actions. Once truth is revealed, it exposes sin. Many hate the truth rather than accepting it. Satan is the reason for hatred while love comes from God.

<u>The Holy Spirit</u> (John 15:26-27)

Jesus promised to send the Holy Spirit as our Comforter and Helper. The Holy Spirit would be greater than Christ had been while on the earth. No one can replace or duplicate the supreme sacrifice Jesus made on Calvary. Jesus' ministry only covered a short distance from His home in Nazareth, but the Holy

Spirit is worldwide since He dwells in every believer's heart. This makes the ministry of the Holy Spirit more widespread than Jesus' ministry that was focused on a small geographic area.

Jesus promised His disciples before sending them out to evangelize the known world in Acts 1:8 by saying, "But ye shall receive power, after that the Holy Ghost (*Holy Spirit*) is come upon you: and ye shall be witnesses unto me both in Jerusalem, and in all Judaea, and in Samaria, and unto the uttermost part of the earth." Jesus dispatched His disciples throughout Asia Minor after they were empowered by the Holy Spirit.

They were sent to preach the gospel message of a risen Savior. As a result, they established many New Testament churches throughout the known world. Their charge was to make disciples, baptizing in the name of the Father, the Son, and the Holy Spirit. They were to teach the message of Christ commanding all people to love one another. Jesus assured the disciples in Matthew 28:20 by saying, "And lo, I am with you always, even unto the end of the world." He was with the apostles then, and He is with each of His children today.

Jesus tells us in Matthew 5:14, "Ye are the light of the world. A city that is set on a hill cannot be hid." We are God's light that shines in a dark world of sin and shame. Love Christ enough to tell others the good news of a risen Savior. Let His light reflect through you to others.

> **I Love to Tell the Story**
> Catherine Hankey, 1866
> "I love to tell the story
> of unseen things above.
> Of Jesus and His glory,
> of Jesus and His love.
> I love to tell the story
> because I know 'tis true.
> It satisfies my longings
> as nothing else can do."

Chapter Seventeen
Christ's Gift

Everyone enjoys receiving a gift. There is a mystique on what is in the box or bag, and we are eager to find out what we have received. There is a lot of excitement at a birthday party or at Christmas time when families gather to meet, eat, and open gifts. The kids rip open their presents as their eyes sparkle with excitement. Sometimes they pay more attention to the gift bag or box than the gift.

There is also excitement when new believers are baptized into Jesus and we receive the gift of the Holy Spirit. Without Christ and the Holy Spirit, we are on the sea of life with no navigation system. The course of our life can quickly change as new circumstances emerge. We may get a new job, get married or divorced, relocate, have children, or tend to aging parents or a spouse until death. These things alter the course in life as we must adjust our priorities. Our change in activities is based on our new circumstances. An advocate is needed to help us navigate the changes we face during these trying times as we don't always have all the answers.

God has given us the gift that does not come wrapped in colorful paper. Jesus was born in a stable (*animal shelter*) and He was wrapped in a newborn infant's swaddling clothes. Before Jesus ascended back to God in heaven, He told His disciples He would send another Comforter. He was referring to the Holy Spirit who is our Helper, Comforter, and Teacher. He can both convict of sin and bless us when we respond favorably to the gospel. He is our partner during our time on earth to help us in all areas of life. We lean on Him to help with our toughest decisions.

When we have a health problem, we see a physician. If we have a tax issue, we use the services of a CPA who knows the tax code. When people encounter stress they cannot handle, they go to a psychologist. We pay these professionals for their services. The Holy Spirit was given to us without charge as He is a gift from God. He is like Jesus, and He will never mislead or lie to us.

This lesson deals with the work of the Holy Spirit, how sorrow can be turned to joy, and some spiritual insight on how to be an overcomer.

A Warning (John 16:1-4)

The Holy Spirit is not a mystical being like a vapor, a genie, or a ghost that floats around to do His work. The Godhead is made up of God the Father, Jesus His Son, and the Holy Spirit. The Holy Spirit is just as real as God or

Jesus. We don't see Him, but through faith we feel His presence.

Jesus revealed to His disciples that what He had told them was not intended to make them stumble in their walk of faith. He warned them they would be put out of the synagogues because of their message of a risen Savior. They would even face death, and their persecutors would mistakenly think they were doing God a service while persecuting the messenger. Their tormentors would do terrible things out of ignorance, as they would not know Jesus or God. He gave them this warning now so the disciples would remember His words when their time came to die for the gospel's sake. They did not always understand what Jesus was saying, but they fully understood Jesus' warning about what lay ahead. Sorrow filled their hearts when they heard Jesus' warning. They were rightfully concerned about their safety as they went out as Christ's ambassadors to preach, teach, and baptize. They had an unbelievable task ahead as they would travel throughout Asia Minor to deliver the message.

From a human perspective, they were not trained for the task. The disciples were common men doing blue collar work when Christ called them. They had not attended seminary to study how to do sermon preparation or plant new churches. When Jesus calls us to do a task, the Holy Spirit empowers us to do an excellent work.

The gift of the Holy Spirit would empower, teach, and encourage the apostles as they scattered into the foreign mission fields. They left their comfortable homes to go to Greece, Turkey, Italy, Samaria, Asia, and other places to carry the message of Christ. They could expect some hostile audiences. The message would be received by many Jews and Gentiles, but they would also be repelled by unbelievers. They could expect threats or even be killed because of their faith in God.

Jesus reassured the disciples that it was to their advantage for Him to go away. If He did not leave them, He would be unable to send their Helper, the Holy Spirt. The Holy Spirit would convict those who did not know Jesus. The disciples were forced to rely on the Holy Spirit as their Helper after Jesus' ascension back to God in heaven.

The Holy Spirit would be their Defender as they struggled in their missionary work and with their warfare against Satan. He does the same for us today. Jesus knew He had laid a heavy burden on the disciples when He warned them of their fate. They were also sorrowful for His upcoming departure in the near future. They naturally wanted Jesus to stay with them because of their friendship and love for Him. The disciples were in mourning and they had a sorrowful fear as they faced the future without Christ by their side. Jesus told them His departure was like a woman in labor. She struggles during delivery, but when the baby is born; her love for the child overrides the pain she suffered. He had many other things to tell them, but they could not bear to hear any more at this time. The Spirit would come and guide them in all truth as they embarked on their mission. He would relay to them the words Jesus would give Him. The Holy Spirit would not be speaking on His own authority but would utter the words Jesus would give Him. The disciples would receive their instructions a little dose at a time so they would not be overwhelmed. The Holy Spirit brings glory to God and to Christ when He speaks to us. Even though we have the Holy Spirit dwelling in our heart, we still have human weaknesses that require His help.

Hope (John 16:5-18)

Jesus needed to lift the disciple's downcast spirits. They needed a reason for hope in spite of the warning of their future fate. Jesus wanted to give them hope when He promised the coming of the Holy Spirit who would help them in His absence. They had not fully accepted the fact that Jesus would die on the cross, so it was probably difficult for them to fully understand the coming of the Holy Spirit. Jesus told them on different occasions that they did not understand what He was saying, but they would in time to come. Their eyes would be opened after His resurrection and ascension back to heaven. Then they would remember Jesus' words and His promises much better.

We may not fully understand all the future events between now and the end-time, but we will fully understand it on the other side. We will see God's plan as it unfolds because we are a part of His plan. When Jesus died and was laid in the tomb, it was sealed. They could no longer see Him, and in fear they went into hiding from the Jews and mourned His death.

Then Jesus came forth in victory from the tomb on the third day after His crucifixion and they rejoiced. He was then with them for forty more days before ascending back to His Father in heaven. Their eyes would be opened to what had happened because they personally witnessed His death and resurrection.

We, too, will come forth in victory over death when Jesus raptures His church. Our earthly bodies will be changed instantly. The corruptible sinful body that was buried will come forth an incorruptible, sinless body that is fit for heaven. Our mortal body that suffered death on earth will be replaced with an immortal body that will never die in heaven. Our eyes will be opened and we will fully understand God's plan that has just been executed. We will finally see Jesus face to face. All sorrows will be turned to joy. We eagerly look forward to the day we meet Jesus face-to-face.

<u>Sorrow Turned to Joy</u>   (John 16:19-24)

The disciples wept and grieved while Jesus was in the tomb, but the world rejoiced over His death. The Jews thought they had finally solved their problems with Jesus when they killed Him. He had been a thorn in their side and they had succeeded when they killed Him; or so they thought. When Jesus rose from the dead, the disciples rejoiced and the world saw what He had said about coming forth from death was true. Now what would Jesus' enemies do with the risen Son of God? Jesus had told His disciples they would scatter like scared sheep when He departed and went back to be with His Father. He was a Master at speaking words of peace, encouragement, and comfort but in this case He issued a warning. He told the disciples in John 16:25, "These things have I spoken unto you in proverbs: but the time cometh, when I shall no more speak unto you in proverbs, but I will show you plainly of the Father."

He told them to be of good cheer and to not be afraid. They must have played these words of Jesus over and over in their minds after His ascension. Now the Holy Spirit could come to be their Helper and Comforter. In this life we must walk through valleys of despair at different seasons. The Holy Spirit is with us in the valleys and in the midst of the storm. He is with us during dark sleepless nights when our problems rob us of sleep. What a wonderful God-given gift we have received from our Lord.

Corrie Ten Boom and her family were all imprisoned and sent to an infested death camp in Germany in World War II. They were mistreated and lived with rats and lice in their meager dorm. There was little food and many starved or froze to death. Corrie was in the lowest pit possible mentally when she said, "No pit is too deep that God cannot reach down with His love and bring comfort in the worst of times." The Holy Spirit and God's love abide with us regardless of our circumstances.

I Am Coming, Lord
Louis Hartsough, 1872
I hear Thy welcome voice,
that called me Lord to Thee,
For cleansing in Thy precious blood
that flowed on Calvary.
I am coming, Lord! Coming now to Thee!
Wash me; cleanse me in the blood
that flowed on Calvary!

Chapter Eighteen
Intercessory Prayers

An intercessory prayer is a prayer we pray for someone else. We often pray intercessory prayers for the sick, the bereaved, for our military personnel, for a lost person who needs Christ, for our church, and possibly even our enemies. The Bible tells us to pray for our enemies. We never know how our prayers can change the attitudes of those who reject God. An intercessory prayer is our plea for someone else to receive a special blessing. You become an earthly advocate when you breathe a prayer on someone's behalf. When we pray for others, our focus shifts from self to those who are in need. One of the most important prayers we pray is for the lost. We want them in heaven instead of being banished from God for eternity.

Jesus prayed for those who arrested, persecuted, and crucified Him. When He was in the process of dying on the cross He prayed in Luke 23:34, "Father, forgive them; for they know not what they do." Jesus had been through two lengthy interrogations throughout Thursday night before He was crucified on Friday. He had been beaten, mocked, battered, and had a crown of thorns pressed down on His brow. The soldiers whipped Him with their cat of nine tails, stripped Him of His garments, and then nailed Him to the cross. As He hung there, He sought God's forgiveness for their ignorance of who He was and His innocence. They did not yet realize He was the Son of God because they refused to believe.

Jesus sits at God's right hand today making intercession for us. Romans 8:34 says, "Who is he that condemneth? It is Christ that died, yea rather, that is risen again, who is even at the right hand of God, who also maketh intercession for us." Jesus didn't forget His disciples when He ascended back to Heaven. He was their Intercessor as He sought God's protection and strength as they carried out a very difficult task.

His love for every person is as strong today as ever. He intercedes for us as our Mediator. His door is open to every person who has not accepted Him as their Lord. Hebrews 7:25 tells us, "Wherefore he is able also to save them to the uttermost that come unto God by him, seeing he ever liveth to make intercession for them." He is faithful as the Intercessor for the saved and unsaved.

<u>Jesus' Prayer for Himself</u> (John 17:1-5)
Jesus' prayer was that He be glorified by God, just as He brought glory to God through His prayers. God delegated and gave Jesus all

power when He came to Earth. Jesus used God's powers by performing miracles that brought glory to His name.

Jesus' time had come to suffer before He was crucified by cruel men. He had finished the work God gave Him to do on Earth. His prayer was that God would glorify Him just as He had done at creation. Christ had to go to the cross and die so He could receive His glorified body when He came forth in victory from the tomb.

Jesus and God have always been completely unified. Jesus glorified God when He went to the cross. His time had now come to carry out God's painful plan. We, too, can glorify God in our suffering. A strong faith is necessary so we can suffer with dignity. We must look through suffering to find God's glory. A suffering person who has a strong faith will not question God but will ask for strength to endure the pain or loss.

Jesus' Prayer for His Disciples (John 17:6-19)
Jesus' disciples were ordinary, common men. They had given up their vocational jobs to follow Christ. Jesus understood their sacrifice when they decided to follow Him. Ordinary people can become strong warriors for Christ when we yield to and fully trust in Him. Jesus showed the disciples the power of

God as He taught and performed many miracles.

They listened intently to Jesus as He taught many parables that showed people their need to follow Him. They witnessed Jesus casting out demons from poor people who were totally controlled by Satan, and they even saw Him raise the dead on several occasions. Jesus did these things to manifest God's power to the people. The disciples were getting the very best on-the-job training Christ could give.

The disciples knew Jesus originated in heaven and His power was given to Him by God. He reminded them several times He did not act on His own authority as He was doing and saying the things that came from the Father. The disciples believed completely in God and Jesus. They did not question when Jesus said repeatedly that God had sent Him to Earth from Heaven.

He knew the challenges His disciples would face when they would go on their missionary trips throughout the known world. Jesus prayed for God to overshadow and keep them in His care as they went. They would face dangerous situations, even life-threating situations, so He prayed they would remain faithful to God when they faced adversity. Jesus wanted their joy to be full when they faced the toughest challenges ever. They could go out in confidence they were doing God's work and carrying out His plan. We, too, can find joy during trying times if we know we are doing what God has called us to do.

The joy of the Lord can come during our times of suffering. Psalms 126:5 says, "They that sow in tears shall reap in joy." We look to God with tear-filled eyes when we suffer knowing the joy of our salvation comes from Him. Joy doesn't come from our bad circumstances, but joy comes from a close relationship with God in the worst circumstances. Our bad circumstances do not define us because we are a child of God.

Jesus loved each disciple and felt they were a gift from God. All twelve men had been faithful to Christ except the one who would betray Him.

Jesus called Judas the son of perdition, meaning the loss of his soul and eternal damnation. Judas brought doom and destruction upon himself when he betrayed Jesus.

The followers of Christ today still face rejection of the gospel message because we are not of this world. We proudly and boldly serve Christ, and unbelievers hate this. When someone rejects the good news of the gospel, they are rejecting God and not the messenger. Rejection by some should give us encouragement to keep telling others about our Lord.

Satan will tempt anyone who is doing the work of God. He will try and get us to lower our standards so the world will like us. It is better to be hated by the world and loved by God. His love reaches from the highest star to the lowest hell. No one can separate us from the love of God.

When the disciples finally went out to preach the gospel and plant New Testament churches, many admired their strong faith and they accepted Christ. New churches sprang up all over Asia Minor due to the work of these ordinary men. Their work was blessed by God in a tremendous way. If you feel unprepared to do something you are asked to do in church, rise to the call. The Holy Spirit will empower you to do what you have been called to do. God works through ordinary people to do His amazing work.

Jesus' Prayer for Believers (John 17:20-21)
Jesus prayed an intercessory prayer when He called on God and said in John 17:20-21, "Neither pray I for these alone *(disciples),* but for them also which shall believe on me through their word; that they all may be one: as thou, Father, art in me, and I in thee, that

they also may be one in us: that the world may believe that thou hast sent me." Jesus asked God to bless the words of the disciples as they preached to unbelievers. He asked God to give unity so all believers can be engrafted in God and Christ. Jesus' prayer was that all who hear will believe He was sent by God to Earth and we see our need for Christ.

In Romans 12:5 we are told, "So we, being many, are one body in Christ, and every one member's one of another." God takes misfits and makes us one in Christ. People from all walks of life come together for worship as one. It doesn't matter what our net worth is, our social standing in the community; or the sins we have committed; we are all one in Christ. There is one faith, one Lord, and one baptism; and we all serve the same Christ (Ephesians 4:5).

Unity in Christ is powerful. The theory of synergy is amazing. Synergy means we can accomplish considerably more by working together as opposed to several individuals working independently. The church family is to work together as a team to accomplish a common goal. Our goal is not fellowship meals or senior trips, although these activities are very enjoyable. The main goal of the church must be the same as Jesus' goal:

that is to seek and to save the lost. Coming together in unity gives us strength. We encourage one another to be involved and be a part of the Lord's work. We should never discourage anyone who wants to contribute their talents to the Lord. God's name is glorified through the unity of believers.

Jesus' benediction for all believers is found in John 17:26, "And I have declared unto them *(believers)* Thy name and will declare it: that the love wherewith Thou hast loved Me may be in them, and I in them." God loves us with an everlasting love (Jeremiah 31:3).

His love never fails in spite of bad circumstances. Jesus told Paul in 2 Corinthians 12:9 when he asked for the thorn to be removed from his body, "My grace is sufficient for thee." God wanted Paul to see how physical weakness can become spiritual strength. Paul realized that he should take pleasure in his infirmities as God would give him the strength needed for his daily walk. God may not remove our problem, but He will give us grace and strength to endure it.

God's love is greater that any disappointment or setback. His grace and mercy enable us to accept His will even in the face of suffering. Peter said in 1 Peter 4:16, "Yet if any man suffer as a Christian, let him not be ashamed; but let him glorify God on this behalf."

Our challenge is to turn our suffering into a blessing for God and others. He made us, He sustains us, and He keeps us in His care.

> **God Will Take Care of You**
> Civilla D. Martin
> Be not dismayed what e'er betide,
> God will take care of you.
> Beneath His wings of love abide,
> God will take care of you.
> God will take care of you,
> through every day, o'er all the way.
> He will take care of you.
> God will take care of you.

Chapter Nineteen
Betrayal, Arrest and Denial

Every government on earth has a fear of betrayal by one of their citizens. Anyone with insider information can betray their homeland and give sensitive information to an enemy nation. This can put national security at risk. A person can be imprisoned for many years, or even executed if they are found guilty of treason or betrayal. There was a man and his wife in New York State who were found guilty in 1953 of giving the USSR some of our sensitive information, and they both died in the electric chair.

Betrayal destroys relationships. A close friend or companion can betray us and do irreparable damage to the friendship. Betrayal can happen in all circles, and it never brings a good result.

Betrayal of Jesus (John 18:1-5)
Jesus and His twelve disciples ate their final Passover meal together on Thursday evening. They reclined around the dining table and enjoyed their meal as they celebrated God's release of their ancestors from 400 plus years of slavery in Egypt many years ago. The Passover Feast was a high holiday for every Jew as they looked back and thanked God for the freedom they found in

Him. The death angel had passed over the Jew's houses and spared the lives of their firstborn. They had every reason to celebrate and thank God for His goodness.

Jesus washed and dried each disciple's feet after supper to give them an example of humble service to follow as they served their fellow man. Judas left the others and went out into the darkness to complete his plan with the soldiers who would arrest Jesus later that evening. Jesus and the other eleven disciples sang a hymn and went out into the darkness. They crossed a ravine at the Kedron Brook and went into a garden.

They were in the garden when Judas arrived with soldiers, guards for the high priests, and Pharisees. They came with lanterns, torches, swords, and clubs as if they were going to arrest a violent criminal. Judas called Jesus Rabbi and kissed Him so the soldiers would know who to arrest. How hypocritical of Judas who had been so close to Jesus for three years to betray Him. He made a mockery of his love for Christ.

Jesus knew what they were planning, so He asked them who they were seeking. Jesus asked them in Matthew 26:50, "Friend, wherefore art thou come?" They told Him they were looking for Jesus of Nazareth. Jesus told them, "I am He." Judas stood nearby with the soldiers. When they arrested Jesus, Peter got so upset that he drew his sword and cut off the ear of Malchus, a servant of the high priest. Jesus touched Malchus' ear and healed him. This was Jesus' final earthly miracle.

What a sad account. Jesus is the innocent Son of God, and Judas was willing to turn on Him. We wonder how Judas felt as he stood with the enemy and heard Jesus say, "I am He." The act had been contrived, the money had been paid to Judas, and now things would go downhill rapidly for both Jesus and Judas. This was the worst betrayal ever and there were no winners.

When we join forces with the enemy, we become one of them. Old friends and values mean nothing so we suddenly think and act like the enemy. Their low morals and standards become ours. Evil associations can only bring bad results. Judas forsook Jesus and joined forces with the enemy.

Caiaphas was the chief priest that year and the Pharisees were the religious elite in the temple. These men were the instigators of the betrayal and arrest. They feared and hated Jesus because of His claims and good deeds. They were jealous they could not perform miracles like Jesus.

They simply could not accept what Jesus said when He repeatedly told them the Father sent Him from Heaven. Fear ruled their hearts as they were concerned the Roman government would take their positions and their government away from them. So they sought to kill Jesus to solve their problem of fear and jealousy.

Hordes of disciples had followed Jesus for three years. They wanted to learn from Him and see His miracles. Judaism was losing their followers to Jesus rapidly and the Pharisees needed to put a stop to it. Many believers stepped outside the box of Jewish tradition to follow Christ.

Jesus' message still draws people to the truth. The message is still as powerful as ever because the truth of the gospel is based on the God-breathed truth from the Bible. His word is anointed and it is powerful enough to cause men to turn from sin to salvation. The message of Christ must never change, for it is the only thing that points lost men to His saving grace.

The church is tempted to become more like the world to attract more people. The church is God's lighthouse to point people whose lives are a shipwreck to Christ. Christians are to be a peculiar people so others want what we have in Christ. Therefore, we must hold the banner of Christ high so the world can clearly see the church is different from the disappointing things of the world.

<u>Arrest and Denial</u> (John 18:12-18)

The soldiers and guards arrested and bound Jesus. They took Him first to Annas, the father-in-law of Caiaphas the high priest. It was Caiaphas that said Jesus must be killed sooner rather than later. Peter and one of his fellow disciples followed Jesus to Annas' house. The other disciple with Peter was recognized by Annas and a girl who kept the door in the courtyard. They knew Peter was a follower of Jesus. The girl asked Peter if he was one of Jesus' disciples. He lied and said he was not a disciple of Christ.

Jesus had told Peter earlier that evening that he would deny him three times before the rooster crowed the next morning. Peter stood by the fire in the courtyard as if he was one of them. He just wanted to keep warm and blend in while he stood with the enemy.

Annas asked Jesus about His disciples and the doctrine He taught. He already knew what Jesus taught, as his son-in-law had suggested Jesus be arrested and killed. Jesus told Annas He had taught openly in the temple, and He had no secrets. Jesus told Annas he should question some of His followers so they could tell him what He taught. One of the officers slapped Jesus with the palm of his hand and warned Him to not answer the high priest like that. Jesus challenged the officer to tell Him what evil He had taught and He asked the officer why he slapped Him.

Annas found no fault in Jesus, so he sent him to Caiaphas for a hearing. He passed the problem to Caiaphas who had recommended Jesus be put to death. Annas knew Jesus was innocent and he wanted no part in killing Him.

As Peter stood by the fire in the courtyard, the Jews asked him again if he was one of Jesus' disciples. Peter lied for the second time and denied being a disciple of Jesus. One of Malchus' relatives had seen Peter cut off Malchus' ear earlier that night in the garden. He was an eye witness that Peter was indeed with Christ; but Peter lied and denied Christ for the third time. Immediately the rooster crowed. Peter departed and wept bitterly.

<u>The Trial</u> (John 18:28-38)

They blindfolded Jesus, mocked, and beat Him. They struck Him in the face again. They demanded that Jesus say who had slapped Him even though He was blindfolded. They spoke many other evil things to Him. Morning finally came to end the awful night He spent before Annas and Caiaphas.

The Sanhedrin council made up of the chief priest and scribes convened on Friday morning to interrogate Jesus. They demanded that Jesus tell them if He was the Christ. Jesus said if He told Him He was Christ they would not believe Him. They then asked Jesus if He was the Son of God and He answered, "You rightly say that I am (Luke 22:70). The council did not find fault in Jesus either, so they referred Him to Pontius Pilate, the governor.

The crowd that followed Jesus to meet with Pilate lied and told Pilate that Jesus had perverted the nation and refused to pay taxes to Caesar. The false witnesses testified that Jesus had said He was Christ, a King. Pilate asked Jesus if He was the King of the Jews. Jesus told Pilate in John 27:11, "Thou sayest." Pilate told the crowd he did not find any fault in Jesus, but the mob got very upset. They refused to accept Pilate's findings.

Pilate knew Herod was in Jerusalem for the Passover Feast. Jesus was from Herod's jurisdiction in Nazareth, so Pilate sent Jesus to Herod for a decision. Herod was glad to meet Jesus for He had heard about the good things He had been doing. Herod wanted Jesus to perform a miracle, but Jesus had not come to perform a miracle. Herod quizzed Jesus, but He would not answer. The people in the crowd got riled up and accused Jesus of several things. The men treated Jesus with contempt and mocked Him. They put a beautiful royal purple robe on Jesus to mock Him because He said He was a king. Herod found no fault in Jesus so he sent Him back to Pilate.

The crowd followed Jesus back to Pilate who told the people again that he found no fault in Him based on their accusations. Annas, Caiaphas, the Sanhedrin council, and Herod had all released Jesus without any formal charges being filed. Jesus had not done anything worthy of death. Pilate said he would chastise Jesus and release Him.

It is customary during the Passover Feast to release one prisoner. The mob demanded that Pilate release Barabbas who had committed murder and kill Jesus instead. Pilate still insisted that he release Jesus, but the crowd cried out in Luke 23:21 "Crucify Him, Crucify Him!" Unfortunately, the people prevailed. Some may feel popular opinion is the best way, but it cost Jesus His life. Pilate finally agreed to sign the order for Jesus to be crucified.

<u>At the Cross</u> (John 19:17-37)

Jesus and two thieves were crucified on Calvary's hill that is called Golgotha in Hebrew. The hill was also called the Place of the Skull because it has the appearance of a skull. There was a thief on either side of Jesus' cross. The soldiers used large iron spikes to nail a criminal to their cross. Pilate provided a sign to go on Jesus' cross in John 19:19 that gave Him the title, "JESUS OF NAZARETH THE KING OF THE JEWS."

They stripped Jesus' garments before nailing Him to the cross. The garments were divided among four soldiers. His tunic was a long outer coat that reached to the hips or below. The soldiers gambled for His tunic. Psalms 22:18 prophesied many years before, "They part my garments among them, and cast lots upon my vesture." Every evil act performed against our Lord had been prophesied hundreds of years earlier in the Old Testament. This included the soldiers gambling for His garments.

One of the prisoners dying on a cross beside Jesus asked Him to remember him when He came into His kingdom. He knew Jesus was innocent and had come from God. He needed forgiveness before he died so Jesus lovingly told him in Luke 23:43, "Today shalt thou be with me in paradise." Hatred could have caused Jesus to be very bitter as He died in pain, but instead He still showed His love and compassion to a thief.

Jesus looked down where He saw John, His beloved disciple and His mother Mary. Jesus told John to take care of His mother; so John took Mary home with him. Apparently Joseph, Jesus' earthly father must have died already and Mary was living alone.

The Scripture was being fulfilled as Jesus died. Jesus said He was thirsty so they put sour wine called hyssop on a sponge and lifted it to Jesus' lips. Jesus cried out loudly in John 23:46, "Father, into Thy hands I commend My spirit: and having said thus, He gave up the ghost." He had breathed his final breath as He gave up His spirit/soul at that moment. The Scriptures that prophesied His death on the cross were now fulfilled.

The soldiers pierced Jesus' side and blood and water drained from His body. He was taken from the cross and buried in a borrowed tomb owned by Joseph of Arimathea, one of the Sanhedrin council members who had disagreed to killing Jesus. The authorities must have thought they had finally solved their problem with Jesus. Little did they know He would rise from death in a couple of days on Sunday. He stayed in the tomb just two nights before coming forth in victory over death and the grave early on the morning of the third day.

Today He sits at God's right hand in the throne room making intercession for each of us. It took His death so we can have everlasting life. Seek a closer walk with Him today.

> **At Calvary**
> William R. Newell
> O the love that drew salvation's plan!
> O the grace that brought it down to man!
> O the mighty gulf that God did span
> at Calvary.
> Mercy there was great and grace was free.
> Pardon there was multiplied to me.
> There my burdened soul found liberty
> at Calvary.

Chapter Twenty
Hallelujah for Our Hope

Death can be perceived as a friend or an enemy. When a patient is suffering with a terminal illness and the pain is off the charts every day and night, we might reluctantly accept death as a friend. There are other instances of a sudden death due to an accident or unforeseen health issue. When a child or young person dies, we consider death as our enemy. The Bible clearly tells us death is our enemy because it separates us from our loved ones.

Jesus had been beaten, battered, and abused before He died on the cross. He suffered several hours on the cross before breathing His final breath. In Mark 16:34, Jesus cried out in agony, "My God, My God, why hast Thou forsaken me?" In John 19:30, Jesus finally said, "It is finished" and breathed His final breath. Death was His friend that delivered Him from unbearable pain. God's plan for Jesus' death was now consummated. The eleven faithful disciples were Jesus' best friends. After He died, they went into hiding as they feared the Jews would also hunt them down and kill them. The morale of these men could not have sunk any lower after Jesus was killed. They mourned and wept in fear.

The disciples heard everything Jesus had said during His ministry and they believed what their limited minds would let them understand. They had been eye witnesses to each miracle and they saw how the miracles changed people's lives in a very positive way. Now Jesus was gone and the disciples mourned. They must have felt defeat as their best friend had died a death He did not deserve.

Joseph of Arimathea sat on the Sanhedrin council. He was there when Jesus was interrogated that Friday morning before being crucified later that day and he did not agree to their decision to kill Jesus.

After Jesus died, Joseph laid Jesus in His new tomb on Friday evening before the Sabbath began at sunset. The tomb was sealed so no one could remove Jesus' body and claim He had been resurrected. It appeared to be over for Jesus. The Pharisees had won and Jesus had lost in death, so it seemed. His earthly suffering and death were over, but God's plan had been fulfilled.

<u>Victory over Death</u> (John 20:1-10)

The Sabbath ended at sunset on Saturday, and it was now before sunrise on Sunday morning. Jesus had been in the tomb since Friday evening. Mary Magdalene and other women came to the tomb early that morning so they could apply spices beneath His burial wrapping. Mark 16:2 said the other women included the other Mary (*mother of James and Jesus*) and Salome. They didn't know how the heavy stone could be moved so they could enter the tomb.

Before they arrived, an earthquake had occurred and the stone was rolled away from the tomb door. The heavy stone had to be removed so the women could get in. However, the stone could have stayed in place and Christ could have exited the sealed tomb since he now had a glorified body that could go through locked doors. The women went in and they saw the undisturbed burial linens and the napkin that had covered His face; but Jesus was not there. The women were confused and perplexed as they couldn't figure out what had happened.

Two angelic men in shining white robes suddenly stood by them. An angel asked the women in Luke 24:5-6, "Why seek ye the living among the dead? He is not here but is risen!" The angel reminded them what Jesus had said earlier that he would be delivered into the hands of sinful men, and be crucified, and the third day rise again. They now remembered Jesus' words, but they could not yet grasp the reality of His resurrection.

Mary Magdalene ran to tell Peter and the beloved disciple what had happened. (*In all likelihood it was John, Jesus' beloved disciple, with Peter*). She told them they had taken away the Lord out of the tomb, and the women didn't know where they have laid him. Luke said the angels at the tomb had just told them Jesus was risen, but the truth had not sunk in. The two disciples ran to the tomb but only Peter went in. He saw the undisturbed burial linens still intact where Jesus' body was wrapped on Friday evening, but Jesus was not there. Jesus had told them earlier that He MUST rise from the dead on the third day, but they had not connected the dots.

His death and resurrection was according to God's plan. Scripture had been fulfilled when Jesus came forth in victory over death. God is more powerful than death, and one day He will abolish it forever.

The Meeting (John 20:11-18)

Mary stood weeping outside the tomb. She turned and saw Jesus standing there but she did not recognize Him. His glorified body did not look like His earthly body that had been buried on Friday evening. Mary thought it was the gardener standing outside the empty tomb. Jesus asked Mary why she was weeping. Mary told Jesus if He had moved

Jesus' body someplace else, she needed to know so she could go to Him. Jesus said, "Mary," and then she recognized His voice. She said "Rabboni" or Teacher. Jesus said to Mary in John 20:17, "Touch me not; for I am not yet ascended to my Father: but go to my brethren, and say unto them, I ascend unto my Father, and your Father; and to my God, and your God." Mary rushed to tell the disciples about seeing Jesus and relay the message He gave her.

<u>Apostles' Commission</u> (John 20:19-23)
A disciple is a learner, but an apostle is one who is sent out like an emissary or a missionary. The twelve disciples had been learners while they traveled with Jesus during His ministry; but now the eleven would be elevated to apostles and become missionaries and church planters.

The disciples were behind locked doors in hiding on Sunday morning for fear of the Jews. Suddenly Jesus appeared among them. He didn't need to knock on the door so someone could open it; He just appeared. They were probably startled this stranger suddenly appeared, so Jesus said, "Peace be with you." They did not know it was Jesus as His appearance had obviously changed. Jesus wanted to give them unquestionable evidence to prove who He was. He showed them His hands and His side where the spikes and spear had pierced His body on Friday. The wounds were healed but the scars were evident.

Thomas was absent when Jesus first appeared with the other disciples on the morning of His resurrection. The disciples later told Thomas they had seen the Lord, but he did not believe them. He said unless he saw the nail prints and put his hand in His side, he would not believe. Thomas must have been overwhelmed by Jesus' cruel death. He may still have been in shock over what they did to Jesus. He simply could not believe Jesus had risen even though he had heard Jesus say He would arise.

Eight days passed, and the disciples, including Thomas, were together. Jesus came through the locked door once again to His disciples. He stood in their midst and said, "Peace to you!" Jesus asked Thomas to inspect His hands and His side so he could believe. Thomas looked and he said in John 20:28, "My Lord and my God."

The presence of Jesus can dispel all fear and doubt if we are willing to believe. Mary, the earthly mother of Jesus proclaimed in Luke 1:37 when she conceived through the work of God and the Holy Spirit thirty-three years previously, "For with God nothing shall be impossible." She conceived through the power of God and the work of the Holy Spirit. The disciples who had been visited by the risen Lord could also easily arrive at the same conclusion, for the humanly impossible had just happened.

After His resurrection, Jesus sent seventy disciples out to preach. He sent them in 35 pairs so they could support and encourage each other. He told them the harvest was great, but the laborers were few. They were instructed to pray for other laborers to come forth. Jesus told them in Luke 10:3, "Go your ways; behold, I send you forth as lambs among wolves." Preachers and missionaries still carry the gospel today into hostile territory.

Just before Christ ascended back to God in heaven, He gave the Great Commission to His disciples. Jesus was getting ready to send these ordinary men out as apostles to the ends of the known world to evangelize and establish New Testament churches. They would do amazing work for the Lord. His charge is recorded in Mark 16:15-16, "Go ye into all the world, and preach the gospel to every creature. He that believeth and is baptized shall be saved; but he that believeth not shall be damned." The apostles would have the privilege of preaching the gospel and baptizing many into Christ. They evangelized and changed the course of all Christendom.

God still uses ordinary people who are willing to step up to the plate when called upon to do His work. Our availability sometimes must exceed our ability. We can do all things through Christ who gives us strength.

These common men went out and changed the world in an uncommon way. They taught, preached, and baptized new believers wherever they went. They made new disciples with the Holy Spirit's help. The Holy Spirit gave them the words to say and the strength to do what they did. They overcame language barriers and local customs to deliver the message of a risen Savior.

Many believed and were baptized as new churches were planted in Antioch, Colossae, Corinth, Ephesus, Galatia, Philippi, Rome, Thessalonica, and other places. The message was preached to both Jew and Gentile and many responded by accepting Christ.

The same message applies today to any person who wishes to receive Christ as the Lord of their life and be baptized in the name of the Father, the Son, and the Holy Spirit.

The Holy Spirit also gave the apostles power to heal the sick and raise the dead. This was the evidence people needed to see so they would know these men were sent by God to do a very special work beyond their human capabilities.

Preachers, teachers, and missionaries who stand without shame or fear to tell others about the love and forgiveness of Jesus need to be encouraged. Their goal is not to have the applause of men; they just want to be God's mouthpiece to a lost generation. These men face rejection and abuse, and they need our prayers.

Today we serve a risen Savior, and that is a Hallelujah fact. We need not fear or doubt who He is; for He came from heaven to earth to save us from our sins. His extreme love and His resurrection give us a living hope of spending eternity with our Lord. We should praise God every day for sending His only Son to redeem us from our sins.

<u>That You May Believe</u>   (John 20:30-31)
There were many signs and miracles Jesus performed in the presence of His disciples. John did not include them all when He wrote the Gospel of John. What he did write gives us the evidence we need to believe through faith. Jesus is the Christ, the anointed and appointed Son of God, and we claim Him as our Savior. We cling to Him and rely upon Him to give us a new life both here and

hereafter. He is the source of life and He lights our way for all to know Him. His light dispels any doubts or fears we may have. His light and the Bible reveal our sins so we can confront them and repent.

Jesus came so we can have an abundant life. His blessings come to us in abundance when we make a commitment to Him. Romans 5:20b tells us, "But where sin abounded, grace did much more abound." God's grace washes away all our sins through the shed blood of Jesus.

In John 5:24, we are told how to be sure we will spend eternity with Christ. "He that heareth my word, and believeth on him that sent me, hath everlasting life, and shall not come into condemnation; but is passed from death unto life." Paul sums it up by saying in Galatians 2:20, "I am crucified with Christ: nevertheless I live; yet not I, but Christ liveth in me: and the life which I now live in the flesh I live by the faith of the Son of God, who loved me, and gave himself for me."

We die to sin and find new life in Christ. We receive new life through His death. Hallelujah for the death, resurrection, and ascension of Jesus. Today He reigns in victory. The Pharisees thought they had won when they killed Jesus, but today He lives! He gave His all for you; will you give your all to

Him? Jesus asks us to surrender our all. That's what He did for us.

> **All to Jesus I Surrender**
> Judson W. Van deVenter
> "All to Jesus I surrender,
> all to Him I freely give.
> I will ever love and trust Him,
> in His presence daily live.
> All to Jesus I surrender,
> humbly at His feet I bow.
> Worldly pleasures all forsaken,
> take me, Jesus, take me now.
> All to Jesus I surrender,
> Lord, I give myself to Thee.
> Fill me with Thy love and power,
> let Thy blessing fall on me.
> I surrender all, I surrender all.
> All to Thee, my blessed Savior,
> I surrender all."

Chapter Twenty-one
The Challenge

It is a good thing to be challenged. New things are learned through a challenge and we can achieve more than expected. Athletes are challenged to be the best in their sport. Students are challenged to set their sights high in their education. Scientists and doctors are challenged to find cures for diseases. Workers are challenged to do more with less. All of us have challenges of some sort in life. Challenges should be seen as opportunities or stepping stones, not roadblocks.

Christians are challenged to live a pure and righteous life before God. We cannot achieve the ultimate walk with God on our strength alone. The Holy Spirit gives us the power we need to keep moving forward. This comes about by meditation on God's Word and spending time in prayer. Then we go do God's work with our families, friends, and in the community.

David's prayer to God in Psalms 51:10 was, "Create in me a clean heart, O God; and renew a right spirit within me." God can renew our hearts to dismiss the things of the world so we will know His will. God gives us a new spirit and attitude when we trust Him.

Ephesians 4:30 says to, "Grieve not the Holy Spirit of God, whereby ye are sealed unto the day of redemption." The Holy Spirit keeps us on the right track as we seek God's will. Our day of redemption is the day Christ will come to rapture His church. He has rescued and freed us as we were slaves to Satan. We find new freedom in Christ, and the Holy Spirit has sealed us with Christ's redemption. Our challenge is to stay connected to God by relying on the Holy Spirit.

John did a wonderful job of writing the biography of Christ while He was here on Earth.

He didn't record everything Christ did, but John gave us a lot of information on why Christ came from heaven to earth, and why His life ended the way it did. Every believer has an assured hope of Jesus' return to rapture His church. There are better days ahead for all believers due to the sacrifice Jesus made for each of us.

<u>Breakfast with Jesus</u> (John 21:1-14)

Seven of the disciples were together on the shore of the Sea of Tiberius one evening. Jesus had risen from the dead and the disciples had seen Him twice before, but they did not immediately recognize Him either time. Jesus' physical appearance had obviously changed after He was resurrected and given a glorified body. Others also saw Jesus after He had risen from the dead, but they did not recognize Him either. Mary, the disciples, Thomas, and the men on the road to Emmaus all had difficulty knowing who He was.

Simon Peter told the other disciples that evening he was going fishing and they said they would join him. They fished all night and caught nothing. They, no doubt, pulled an empty net in all night. Morning came and Jesus stood on the shore, but the disciples still did not know Him. He asked them if they had any meat, but all they had was an empty net.

Jesus told them to cast the net on the right side of the boat, and they would find fish. They did as Christ said and caught so many fish they couldn't pull the net into the boat. John then recognized Jesus and told Peter who it was standing on the shore. The other disciples pulled the net full of fish to the shore using a smaller boat.

Jesus had built a fire on the sand and cooked bread and fish for the disciples. He told them to bring some of their fish they had just caught. They counted 153 large fish in the net, but miraculously the net did not break. Jesus invited them to sit and eat breakfast on the beach.

The disciples now knew it was Jesus who asked them to eat, just as it was He who told them to cast their net on the right side of the boat. He served the bread and fish to His disciples just as He served them earlier at the Last Supper. Jesus' visit that morning met both a physical and spiritual need for the disciples.

Jesus' Challenge to Peter (John 21:15-19)
Peter denied knowing Christ three times the night He was betrayed by Judas Iscariot. His denial was still fresh in Jesus' mind. Jesus could have criticized Peter for his triple denial, but instead He used the occasion to bolster and restore Peter's confidence and faith. He lifted Peter up to a new level of commitment instead of causing him to be burdened with guilt. Christ had a very important mission in mind for Peter and he needed all the encouragement and motivation Jesus could give.

The disciples finished eating breakfast. It was now time for Jesus to ask Peter a very simple but piercing question. He asked Peter three times in John 21:15-17,"Simon, son of Jonas, lovest thou me more that these? He saith unto him, 'Yea, Lord; thou knowest that I love thee.' He saith unto him, "Feed my lambs." He knew Peter loved his fellow disciples, but Christ wanted him to confess his superior love for Him. Peter told Jesus all three times he loved Him, and Jesus responded by telling him each time to feed His lambs and His sheep.

Jesus knew Peter's weakness. Most of the time there was no question about Peter's love for Jesus; but after denying Him three times, he needed to reaffirm his love for Him. The reason this was so important is because he was to be designated as the preacher who would soon speak to Jesus' murderers on the upcoming Day of Pentecost.

On the Day of Pentecost, Peter boldly preached to the Jews who killed Jesus on the cross. When Peter confronted them with their crime against Christ, they asked in Acts 2:37 what they needed to do. They didn't know what to do to make things right. Peter told them in Acts 2:38, "Repent, and be baptized every one of you in the name of Jesus Christ for the remission of sins, and ye shall receive the gift of the Holy Ghost."

Three years earlier, John the Baptist had baptized Jesus when His ministry was launched, and the Holy Spirit descended at that time on Jesus in the form of a dove. Three years after Jesus was baptized, Peter told these Jews on the Day of Pentecost they should be baptized for remission of sins and receive the gift of the Holy Spirit. There is a divine pattern of the Holy Spirit coming to us when we are baptized.

In John 21:18, Jesus forewarned Peter of the persecution he would face when he went out to preach the gospel. He told Peter that when he grew old, others would carry him where he did not want to go. Jesus was referring to the persecution Peter and the other disciples faced. It would be through their death as martyrs that God's name would receive glory. Jesus told Peter to follow Him.

Are we as ready as Peter and the other disciples to follow Jesus? Are our love and faith strong enough to enable us to make a commitment and carry it out regardless of the challenges? Peter told Jesus he would follow him to death, but then denied Him three times the night Jesus was betrayed. We cannot ignore the question regarding the strength of our own faith. Christ expects our loyalty to the end of the way.

<u>Jesus' Challenge to Us</u>

The disciples paid a heavy price for their discipleship to Christ. They went out boldly and preached the Word of God. They faced strong opposition from the Pharisees and others.

They were beaten and thrown in jail. Eventually, ten of the eleven apostles died a martyr's death, except John who was exiled to a remote island. The Apostle Paul, who was not one of the original disciples but also became an apostle, was imprisoned and eventually beheaded. The cost of their discipleship was horrendous, but they served bravely to their deaths.

Jesus gives us the cost of our discipleship in five New Testament verses.

- Matthew 16:24: we must deny self and carry our cross
- Luke 14:26: our love for Christ must be deeper than our love for family members or a spouse
- Luke 14:33: we must be willing to forsake all to be His disciple
- John 8:31: always follow Jesus' word
- John 15:8: we must bear much fruit to bring glory to God

The cost of our discipleship to Christ requires self-denial and cross-bearing. We must elevate our love for Christ above all others. Christ must be more important than possessions or other earthly things. Staying faithful to the Word of God is critical in our bearing much fruit for Him. Salvation cost

Jesus His life; likewise, our discipleship costs us to follow Him and do His work.

Jesus also teaches us to serve Him openly and with boldness. There is no place for secret discipleship. Nicodemus, many Jews, and Joseph of Arimathea all tried to follow Him secretly. Christ served mankind openly, and He expects no less from us. If we confess Him openly before men, He promised in Luke 12:8 He will confess us before God.

Paul spoke bravely when he said in Romans 1:16, "For I am not ashamed of the gospel of Christ; for it is the power of God unto salvation to everyone that believeth; to the Jew first, and also to the Greek." Paul was always bold in his witness for the Lord.

He proclaimed God's mercy and grace to both Jews and Gentiles. He preached about the power of God to save men lost in sin so they can receive salvation. Jesus is our only way to God. It took death on the cross so Jesus can be our way to God.

When God controls our life we need not be ashamed of proclaiming His name to anyone who will listen. Hebrews 4:12 tells us, "For the Word of God is quick, and powerful, and sharper that any two-edged sword, piercing even to the dividing asunder of soul and spirit, and of the joints and marrow, and is a discerner of the thoughts and intents of the heart." The power of God's word should never be questioned. It can pierce hardened hearts that have rejected Christ for many years.

As we meditate on the scriptures, we learn of the power contained in the Bible. The Word of God works through the Holy Spirit to convict us of sin so we can find forgiveness. It is sharp and can pierce guilty hearts, as it causes us to examine our actions, thoughts, and the intents of our heart. Then the Holy Spirit can lead us into a proper relationship with God.

The Bible tells us of the spiritual weapons we have with which to fight Satan and his angels. The scriptures and the Holy Spirit equip us for warfare with Satan. The Bible is our sword as we fight and firmly resist Satan. We need the scriptures to give us the faith, strength, and stamina needed for our battle against evil. We must watch like a military sentry and stand fast in our faith to be an effective soldier. We are told throughout the Bible to be bold and not fear, for God is with us in our times of temptation and trials.

Paul said in Ephesians 6:10, "Finally my brethren, be strong in the Lord and in the power of His might." God's child never needs to feel weak or insufficient as God is our Refuge and Strength. He is with us in our times of trouble and will never forsake us. Every person must decide how closely they want to follow Christ. We can follow Him closely or afar off. Our relationship with Christ can be as strong as we desire. He wants us to follow Him closely every day.

James Sammis wrote a hymn that says in part, "Trust and obey, for there's no other way to be happy in Jesus, but to trust and obey."

Benediction
Numbers 6:24-27
May the LORD bless thee, and keep thee:
May the LORD make his face to shine upon thee, and be gracious unto thee:
May the LORD lift up his countenance upon thee and give thee peace.
Amen

Introduction to Peter
The Apostle Peter's Two Epistles (Letters)

Peter wrote two letters to dispersed Jews who believed in Jesus as God's Son and to Christians worldwide. His letters had two main themes:
- Victory over suffering just as Christ suffered.
- An alert regarding false teachers and how we counteract them by being grounded in God's Word.

Peter tells about the living hope in Jesus who brings salvation to all who elect to believe and receive Him as Lord. When we accept Jesus we have an eternal inheritance promised.

We are to live righteous and pure lives before God because of what Jesus, our sacrificial Lamb, did for us on the cross. Christians are like pilgrims in this world who are to live with honor and in holiness before God and man.

Christians are called to suffer for righteousness' sake, and this gives us reason to rejoice that we can suffer for our Lord. We must be on guard for false teachers who would lead us away from God if we don't resist them. The elders of the local church are the gatekeepers to silence all false teachers and protect the church, the bride of Christ.

Scripture verses quoted are from The Amplified Bible (AMP).

Chapter Twenty-two
The Sure Foundation

In John 1:40-43, Jesus launched His three-year ministry on earth. He called twelve disciples to leave their vocational jobs and work with Him in His ministry. Their ministry was limited to an area that did not exceed 200 miles, the distance from Judea in the south to Galilee in the north.

Before Jesus called any disciples, He met with John and Andrew to get acquainted. The two men spent the day with Jesus. Andrew quickly concluded Jesus was the Messiah that God had sent from heaven to earth. It was about four o'clock in the afternoon when Andrew went to Simon Peter, his brother. Andrew told Peter in John 1:41, "We have found the Messiah, which translated is Christ, the Anointed One." Jesus was anointed and appointed by God to come to earth so He could show people how to receive forgiveness for their sins.

When Andrew brought Peter to Jesus, He told Peter in John 1:42, "You are Simon son of Jona, you shall be called Cephas, which translated means a stone."

In Matthew 16:13-19, Jesus was in Caesarea Philippi after calling His disciples. He asked them, "Who do people say that I the Son of

Man am?" They told Jesus some thought he was John the Baptist, Elijah, or Jeremiah. There was not a consensus among the people on who Jesus really was. It is understandable how they might think He was a prophet. They had been exposed to or taught about prophets previously, so it was easy for some to make an assumption that Jesus was a prophet.

Jesus then asked His disciples, "But who do you say that I am?" Peter answered, "You are the Christ, the Son of the living God." Jesus heard what He needed to hear. At least one disciple understood who He really was.

<u>The Foundation of the Church</u>

Jesus' response to Peter is recorded in Matthew 16:17-19 that says, "Blessed (*happy*) are you Simon Bar-Jona; for flesh and blood (*men*) have not revealed this to you, but My Father who is in heaven. And I tell you, you are Peter (*Greek: Petros, a large piece of rock*). I will build my church, and the gates of Hades (*the powers of the infernal region*) shall not overpower it. I will give you the keys of the kingdom of heaven; and whatever you bind (*declare to be improper and unlawful*) on earth must be what is already bound in heaven; and whatever you loose (*declare lawful*) on earth must be what is already loosed in heaven." The truth Peter spoke about Christ being the Messiah was the rock upon which Christ would build His church.

The church is not built on shifting sand or unstable soil, for it has a solid foundation which is Christ our Lord. Satan and all his fallen angels may attack the church, but it will stand to the end of time. Some may fall away due to unbelief or conflicts, but the church will survive. The truth does not change with prevailing conditions. God's people who have accepted Christ as their Lord are His church. The church is not a building, but it is the faithful believers who gather for worship of their Almighty God.

When we accept Christ, we become a part of His body and collectively we make up the church. The body of Christ, the church, must work together in unity just as our physical bodies. If one of our major organs fails, the entire body is affected. The same is true in the church; if one person fails to perform their role, the entire church is impacted.

Jesus taught a parable about the vine and the branches in John 15. The branches (*believers*) are connected to the vine (*Jesus*) so we can bear much fruit for the Lord. The branches are the fruit-bearers, not the vine.

We demonstrate goodness, kindness, mercy, patience, etc. which are some of the fruits we are expected to produce as God's child. By working together as a team, the entire church gains strength and is more fruitful for the Lord.

Eternal Inheritance (1 Peter 1:1-12)

Peter wrote his epistle (*letter*) to the believers in at least five different locations. They had one thing in common even though they were scattered. They all believed in Jesus as the Son of God. Their sins had been washed away through the shed blood of Jesus.

Peter first gave praise to God. It was by God's unlimited mercy that Peter and his fellow believers had been born again to a living hope. This hope resulted from the resurrection of Jesus on the third day after He was crucified. Peter told the dispersed believers they had been born afresh and given an inheritance that is beyond the reach of change and decay. Our hope is eternal and it will not fade with time or circumstances. It won't perish because it is reserved for us in heaven.

Our trust is in God who will guard our faith and hope like a military sentry. When we arrive in God's presence after this life is over, He will reward us with our inheritance. Our final salvation will then be fully revealed so we can spend eternity with our loving Father. God is looking forward to our coming to Him in the New Jerusalem just as much as we yearn for that day.

In the meantime, we are on earth and are distressed with the conditions around us. Evil is rampant since many want to bring harm to themselves and others. Pride, greed, murder, rape, disagreements, conflicts/war, and many other problems must be endured on our spiritual journey. One day God will utterly wipe the earth clean of all signs of sin and all things will be made new. Then we can live at peace with our heavenly Father. This unhappy life will be transformed to a happy and peaceful life forever.

Our faith is tested with all the problems on earth. At times we may not even know how to pray for relief. The Holy Spirit can take our groaning and turn it into a beautiful prayer to God (Romans 8:26). Faith is essential to a successful walk with God.

Faith is more precious than gold that has been tested in fire. When our faith is tested to the extreme, it is purified and made stronger. It is faith that enables us to withstand the evil works of the devil. We rely on God to lead us through every problem of life. He has promised to never leave or forsake us during the storms of life.

One day we will see Jesus when He is revealed to us for the first time. We don't see Him now, but we believe and love Him. This relationship is one of faith and not sight. Knowing Christ is our risen Lord gives us reason to rejoice and be glad. Salvation is the benefit we receive by accepting Christ as our Lord. Salvation brings our faith to fruition and reality.

The prophets in the Old Testament searched for and inquired about salvation. They could not find salvation since it comes from Christ. The coming Messiah had been foretold and prophesied, but He had not come yet. His coming and His suffering were foretold by the prophets hundreds of years before Christ was born. They continued in faith looking for the Messiah to come. They hoped they would still be living when He finally came.

The prophets left an example for us to follow today. They had a strong faith in someone they had never seen. His coming had been revealed to them and this gave them a strong faith He would actually come someday. We too await the coming of Christ when He will rapture the church and take us home to be with Him. We have a strong hope and this is cause for rejoicing. The promise of His coming gives us the joy and hope of our salvation.

<u>Living in Hope</u> (1 Peter 1:13-21)

Hope is what keeps us going during the trials of life. Hope gives us reason to believe better things and better days are ahead. Hope in Christ is a spiritual hope that reaches beyond this world. We can live in hope or despair.

The Apostle Paul tells us in Romans 8:24, "For in hope we are saved. But hope which is seen is not hope. For how can one hope for what he already sees?" Hope enables us to believe in something we cannot touch or see. We cannot see Jesus but through hope and faith we feel His presence.

Hope is what carries us through adversity. Paul said in 2 Corinthians 4:8, "We are pressed (*troubled and oppressed*) in every way, but not crushed; we suffer embarrassments and are perplexed and unable to find a way out, but not driven to despair; we are pursued, but not deserted; we are struck down, but never struck out or destroyed." Paul had experienced the hard knocks of life when he was ship wrecked, beaten, and imprisoned; but none of these terrible things shook his faith and hope in the Lord. He was finally removed from his chains in a prison in Rome and beheaded for the sake of Christ.

Paul knew what would happen after this life is over, and this increased his hope. He said he preferred to be with the Lord. He tells us that when we are present in the body we are absent from the Lord; but when we abandon our earthly body, we are present with the Lord (2 Corinthians 5:7-8). All of earth's problems will be over when we are with the Lord forever.

Hope encourages and inspires clean living. 1 John 3:3 says, "And everyone who has this hope cleanses (*purifies*) himself just as He is pure (*guiltless*)." Believers are cleansed by the blood of Christ. Once our sins are washed away, we move forward to serve Christ, not Satan. We are not to turn back to sin once we have named Christ as our Lord. We move forward in the hope of being with Him soon.

We are to brace our minds, be morally alert, and set our hope entirely on God's grace that will fully come to us when Jesus is revealed. We are to be obedient children of God, and not go back to the evil desires that ruled our lives when we lived for Satan. We were ignorant to the things of God then, but now we know the truth of the Gospel.

God, who called us out of sin, is holy and He requires holy and clean living from His children. God said in Leviticus 11:45, "Therefore you shall be holy, for I am holy."

When we accept Christ, we also accept God's standards for living. We are no longer to be conformed to this world after accepting Christ.

We are temporary residents on earth while we prepare to live forever in the New Jerusalem. God expects us to be committed fully to Him during our time on earth, regardless of how long we might live. Life is fragile and uncertain, so we need to live every day as if it is our last day on earth.

Christ has redeemed and rescued us from our former life of sin and disobedience. The environment in which we grew up may influence the direction we take in life. As we grow spiritually we can make choices on whether we want to be trapped in a bad situation that leads nowhere or rise above our upbringing to a much better life. No one is bound to the bad decisions of parents. We can be born again to a new life with Christ.

Christ purchased our salvation with His blood. He paid our sin debt in full when He died on the cross. He became our sacrificial Lamb so we can be saved from our sins. Jesus was perfect and sinless, but He took our sins upon Himself when He died in our place. The cross was Jesus' destiny before creation. It was God's plan for Jesus to die in our stead. Our faith and hope is in God who raised His

Son from death in victory. God has brought glory and honor to Jesus for what He did on the cross. Our faith and hope rest in God.

Peter tells us in 1 Peter 1:24-25, "For all flesh (*mankind*) is like grass, and its glory (*honor*) like the flower of grass. The grass withers and the flower drops off. But the Word of the Lord endures forever. And this Word is the good news which was preached to you." This life ends quickly just as the rose only blooms for a short period. It is beautiful while it is in full bloom, but its beauty quickly fades. Life is like the rose. Make your life count for God.

Chapter Twenty-three
The Chosen Stone

Every believer wants to be a learner or a disciple of Christ. The more we know about His mercy, grace, and forgiveness, the more we want to know. We learn about His compassion from His example, words, and actions. Christ is our pattern for living a successful Christian life. When we imitate Jesus, we will automatically do good deeds that encourage strong relationships. Even though Christ went about doing good deeds, many despised what He did. They could not heal the sick or raise the dead nor could they cast out demons or touch blinded eyes and give a person sight. We, too, may be hated or shunned for the work we do for the Lord even though our work can never equal Christ's.

Envy and jealousy are strong evil forces in our world. When you do something commendable, an on-looker may envy what you did and wish they could do the same thing. Because of their circumstances or relationship with the Lord, it may be impossible for them to duplicate your good deeds. Envy can turn into jealousy. These are tools of Satan that can hamper our effectiveness in doing Christ's work. They also do irreparable damage to relationships. Other people's desires or opinions do not lessen the need for our full commitment to Christ.

Paul wrote in Colossians 1:10, "That you may walk (*live*) in a manner worthy of the Lord, fully pleasing to Him and desiring to please Him in all things, bearing fruit in every good work and steadily growing and increasing in and by the knowledge of God." Paul is saying the Christian walk begins with our attitude. We desire to please the Lord and want to bear fruit through good works and by gaining more knowledge of Him. The more we know about Christ, the more successful we will be in His work. Good works bring honor to our gracious Savior.

<u>Shun Evil</u> (1 Peter 2:1-3)

Christians are to be pro-active and shun evil. We must be like Christ and resist Satan with vigor to be able to do God's work. Until we deal with evil, we cannot be effective on our personal walk or in reaching others. 1 Corinthians 10:6 tells us, "Now these things are examples (*warnings*) for us not to desire or crave or covet or lust after evil and carnal things." The warning tells us we have two options: serve Satan and do evil deeds or serve Christ and do good deeds. Craving or lusting robs us of a close relationship with Christ.

The apostle says in 1 Peter 2:1 that we must be done with every trace of wickedness, deceit, and insincerity (*pretense, hypocrisy*). Grudges (*envy and jealously*), slander, and evil speaking are not Christ-like fruits. We cannot serve Christ and Satan at the same time. We must choose who we want as the higher being, or the lord of our life. By shunning Satan, we are also shunning evil. Paul said in 1 Thessalonians 5:22, "Abstain from evil (*shrink from it*) in whatever form or whatever kind it may be." We are to take the high road and stay aloof from evil. This strengthens our relationship with Christ and allows us to focus on doing good deeds. It is up to us to take the first step to shun Satan and his evil works.

Peter's list of evils in 1 Peter 2:1 is extensive. Most likely, at least one of these evils may be one of our problems. The bottom line is that we must shun all evil or the appearance of evil to be able to do our utmost for Christ.

A Christian is like a newborn baby who craves milk. We should be craving and desiring earnestly the pure spiritual milk found in God's Word. Only when we receive spiritual nourishment can we grow in Christ. When we accept Christ, we get a taste of the good things He offers. We automatically grow spiritually when we feed on God's Word and apply it to our lives. It should be our desire to grow in Christ as we progress to spiritual maturity.

Jesus' desire is that we not remain as spiritual babes but grow up in Him so we can contribute to His cause. This maturity allows us to act and behave in a manner pleasing to the Lord. As we grow into spiritual maturity, we can stand on our own feet with the help of the Holy Spirit to defend our faith in Christ.

<u>A Chosen Stone for a Chosen People</u> (1 Peter 2:4-10)

During Jesus' time on earth some looked at Him as a living stone while others inspected what He did and rejected Him. Some followed Him for a while and then turned away. Jesus is precious in God's sight and He is loved immensely by His followers.

There was a stone dealer in Italy many years ago. He bought and sold large stones for sculpturing. He had one stone on his yard that sat there for a long time. Men would look at it but all they saw was a stained jagged hunk of rock; there was no outward beauty and they could not see any potential. One day, a man stood for a long period and gazed at the stone and he envisioned something beautiful inside. He bought the stone and sculpted an amazing piece of art. This is how some viewed Jesus. There was no outward beauty but the potential with Christ is unlimited. He can take our sinful life and sculpt it into something beautiful if we let Him.

God calls us today to be living stones that can be built into a strong spiritual house. We are to give God our best so we can offer spiritual sacrifices that are acceptable and pleasing to Him. We bring God offerings of worship and praise to thank Him for His goodness and provision. In the Old Testament, people offered physical sacrifices to reconcile with God and today we offer ourselves as a sacrifice.

Hebrews 13:15 tells us, "Do not forget or neglect to do kindness and good, to be generous and distribute and contribute to the needy, for such sacrifices are pleasing to God." When we help someone who has real needs, we come into a closer fellowship with God.

A cornerstone or a setting stone has been used by architects and builders for centuries. The Egyptians used large cornerstones at each corner of a pyramid. Cornerstones are used to design and construct large temples, cathedrals, and other important buildings around the globe. The cornerstone is the first stone laid on the foundation. The stone is selected carefully for its strength and durability as it will be a load-bearing stone. The cornerstone is important because it keeps a building square and straight.

Jesus is the Christian's cornerstone. He is our rock that will endure for our lifetime and throughout eternity. Jesus bore the load of sin for all mankind when He went to the cross to die in our place. He is our loving Savior who forgives our sins when we fall short.

The Old Testament prophet said in Isaiah 28:16, "Therefore says the Lord God, 'Behold I am laying in Zion for a foundation a Stone, a tested Stone, a precious Cornerstone of sure foundation: he who believes will not be ashamed or give way or hasten away (*in panic*).'" This verse is repeated in 1 Peter 2:6. God sent His Son to be the foundation stone for all mankind. He has been tested with temptations, trials, and death on the cross; a death He did not deserve. When we place our trust in Christ and believe He is God's Son, we should never be ashamed. He is our Savior and we are to proudly and boldly proclaim Him as our Lord.

Men have rejected Christ as the Cornerstone for eons, but God carefully selected Him before creation to be the foundation stone for our spiritual house. He is a stumbling stone and an offensive stone to disbelievers, but He is our stepping stone to eternity.

1 Peter 2:9 says we are a chosen race, a royal priesthood and a dedicated nation. God has chosen every person who will accept His gift of forgiveness through Jesus Christ. Our salvation was purchased by the shed blood of Jesus.

Christians are called to God's priesthood to humbly serve others. We are dedicated by Him to do His special work for humanity. He has called us out of the darkness of sin to emulate Christ though our commitment to Him and faithful service to others. We are to serve those in need as we serve Christ.

Believers are special people in the sight of God. He calls us His people because He has purchased us through Jesus' sacrifice. He is our God and we are His child. What a blessing to be called a child of God. He has so many good things in store that will be revealed one day to all His children.

God calls us to a pure and holy life, just as He is holy. We are like aliens and strangers in this world. God expects us to abstain from evil desires and passions of the flesh that wage war against our souls. We are to take the high road when others criticize and slander us for being a Christian. God sees what is going on in your life. You can rest assured there will eventually be a day of reckoning for both the believer and unbeliever. The Christian will be rewarded for their good deeds on earth and the unbeliever will be condemned and banished from God forever. God looks out for you like a shepherd who loves and cares for His sheep.

<u>Submission</u> (1 Peter 2:13-25)

Believers expel Satan and accept Christ as Lord. We submit to Christ the same as a military recruit submits to their commanding officer. When a recruit takes the oath to uphold the constitution and obey the Commander-in-Chief, he or she is temporarily giving up all they own to become a member of one of our military branches.

Their commanding officer directs their life at every level. They tell the recruits when to get up and when to bed down. The recruit is told when, where, and what to eat.

They surrender hair styles and wardrobes so they can be an acceptable soldier, sailor, or airman. Their life of freedom is now one of submission to the military.

We are to be willing to submit to the government and our masters. Man has proven he cannot self-govern, so we live in a land of laws. The law allows us many freedoms so we can enjoy life without fear of an arrest. However, we must respect the law and the leaders who enacted them, even when we don't agree. This is the only way a society can survive and thrive.

The Apostle tells us in 1 Peter 2:13-14, "Be submissive to every human institution and authority for the sake of the Lord, whether it be to the emperor as supreme, or to governors as sent by him to bring vengeance (*justice*) to those who do wrong and to encourage those who do good service." Obedience to the laws of the land brings honor to God. If we don't like what our leaders are doing, we will have the opportunity to vote for a new leader in the next election. In the meantime, we are expected to be law-abiding citizens.

It is God's will and intention that by doing right we will silence the ignorant charges and ill-informed criticisms of foolish persons. When we obey the law, we live freely to do the things God tells us. We live to please our Father and at the same time live within the law.

God's charge to us is to show respect for everyone and treat them with honor. The Golden Rule tells us to treat others as we want to be treated (Matthew 7:12). The world would be a much better place if every person simply followed and practiced the

Golden Rule. We are to love all other believers over which Christ is the head, reverence God, and obey the leaders of the land.

In Bible times, the wealthy had servants that worked in their homes. Peter admonishes household servants to honor and respect their masters whether they were just or unjust. Masters can treat their servants humanely or they can take advantage and abuse them. Regardless, servants are told to respect their masters. This may mean enduring the pain of unjust suffering.

We serve Christ who is our Master. We may be doing the right thing but find it necessary to suffer patiently for His sake. If we suffer with dignity the things we feel we do not deserve, Christ is honored and pleased. We are called to suffering just as Christ suffered. Jesus was not guilty of any sin or crime, but He suffered because God wanted Him to be our example in how we are to bear up under suffering.

Jesus was criticized and insulted, but He did not retaliate. They slapped Jesus in the face and spit in His face before they crucified Him, but He took it like a man. He was abused and suffered, but He did not threaten His abusers. Jesus simply trusted in God for deliverance from these evil men who inflicted so much undeserved pain.

Jesus bore our load of sins all the way to the cross. His body was offered up to God as a sacrifice. The cross became Jesus' sacrificial altar. He died for us so we can die to sin and live righteously and victoriously before God. Peter said in 1 Peter 2:24b-25, "By His wounds you have been healed. For you were going astray like so many sheep, but now you have come back to the Shepherd and Guardian of your souls." The Shepherd Jesus leads and guards His children throughout life. He gives us strength to stand in the face of adversity so we can honor God.

Remember the instructions Paul gives in Colossians 1:10: "That ye walk (live) in a manner worthy of the Lord, fully pleasing Him."

Chapter Twenty-four
Submission

No one likes the idea of submitting to others. When we submit, we lose our freedom and become sub-servient. Every person probably looks at themselves as being able to make their own decisions without asking permission. Freedom to act is a wonderful gift, but with the freedom comes accountability. We are all accountable to each other and more importantly, to God. Therefore, it is good to know His plan and framework for living as a family unit and a Christian.

Even the CEO of a major corporation must submit to the will of others. He or she must produce operating and profit results that please their board of directors and shareholders. All of us from the least to the greatest must submit to other people and to God. Our minds must be conditioned to this fact as submission is not natural.

A five-star general in the military must submit to the wishes of the President of the United States who is the Commander-in-Chief. Even the President submits to the will of the people or risk losing the next election. As Christians, we are to submit our lives to God. "So be subject to God. Resist the devil (*stand firm against him*), and he will flee from you (James 4.7)." We submit to God so He can empower us to stand firm against Satan as he deceives and lies to lead us astray. God is faithful to supply all our needs including the strength to fight Satan.

In 1 Peter 3, he talks about wives being submissive to their husband, but this places extra accountability on the husband to act according to God's will. God never intended for the wife to become a battering target, either verbally or physically. The husband and wife each have their God-given assigned duties in marriage. Mutual love and respect must prevail daily for the marriage to be healthy and enduring.

<u>Duty of the Wife</u> (1 Peter 3:1-6)

Peter says the wife must be subordinate to her husband. She is to depend on her husband to protect and provide the family's needs. The wife adapts so she fits within this framework that God established. If a husband has not accepted Christ, the wife is not to preach and nag, but instead live a godly life so He will see Christ in her. This pattern of behavior works in real life. Some wives may be a godly example to their unbelieving husbands for years before they finally accept Christ.

This can also work in reverse if the husband is a Christian and the wife isn't. Patience is required for the seed to bear fruit. The ideal situation is for the man and his wife to both accept Christ before marriage, but unfortunately this does not always work.

The wife is to be pure and modest in the way she behaves. She is to show respect for her husband and defer to him. She is to esteem and appreciate him as long as he does not take advantage. A wife is to love and adore her husband according to 1 Peter 3:2. This adoration and love are to be sincere and genuine and not be for an outward show. She is to not overly adorn herself with expensive jewelry and trips to the salon when the family is struggling to make ends meet financially.

The wife is to adorn her inward self with the beauty of God. When God reigns in her heart, the wife will have no problem doing what God commands. She is to have charm and promote peace in the family. She will try and bring peace when voices are being raised. She will try to be a peace-maker when there are differences of opinion.

In some foreign cultures, women's rights are scarce. In the past, women were not allowed to drive and they walked a few paces behind their husbands to show his leadership role.

Marriage is a partnership and it seems that God expects us to walk hand-in-hand as partners to encourage and uplift one another. This is how two people can be united and become as one. While the husband is to take the lead, he is not to act in a dictatorial manner with his wife.

Peter had a reason for addressing the subject of submission to husbands and wives. In the Old Testament, women beautified their outward appearance for their husband. They adapted their life to serve their husband's needs. Sarah followed Abraham's guidance by calling him lord (master and leader). Women are encouraged to follow Sarah's example without fear.

1 Peter 3:7 lets husbands know how they should behave for their wife's benefit. He said, "In the same way you married men should live considerately with your wives, with an intelligent recognition of the marriage relation, honoring the woman as physically the weaker, but realizing you are joint heirs of the grace of life, in order that your prayers may not be hindered and cut off. (*Otherwise, you cannot pray effectively*"). The husband is to show consideration to his wife with a clear understanding of the marriage relationship. He is to honor her and realize both the husband and wife can

equally claim God's grace. This attitude is essential if the husband wants his prayers answered.

Joint Responsibilities (1 Peter 3:8-12)

According to the Center for Disease Control, the divorce rate in America in 2000 was 49%. This rate would fall tremendously if every couple could agree on God's requirements in marriage prior to saying, "I do." They would be much better off not marrying if they could not agree on these instructions from God.

What does God have to say to couples? The husband and wife have certain God-given responsibilities to each other. Peter lists specific actions that are a requirement of God. They should show mutual compassion, be united in mind and spirit, sympathizing with one another, loving each other, courteous, tenderhearted, and humble. If Christ reigns in our heart, we have no problem accepting any of these assigned responsibilities.

There is no place in marriage to return evil for evil or insult for insult. We have been called instead to pray for one another because we are concerned for our partner's welfare and happiness. When we follow God's call, He will bless us with His protection in our marriage. We are to control our tongues from speaking evil or deceit to our partner. There is a pledge of love and support at the marriage altar, and this is according to God's plan. Selfish ambitions are to be forfeited when we come together as one in marriage.

Each partner is to turn away from wickedness. We are to eagerly seek peace that brings happiness to our home. 1 Peter 3:11 instructs us to aggressively seek peace and happiness.

David gives some instructions for all Christians in Psalms 34:12-15. These verses reach beyond marriage to every believer. He is teaching us as little children on some basic requirements of God. We are to keep our tongue from evil and our lips from speaking deceit; we depart from evil to do good works. We should be hungry for peace and pursue it. He tells us God looks down on those who practice righteousness without compromise. He has promised to hear the prayers of the righteous. We would all do well to heed these instructions from God.

<u>Suffering for the Right Reasons</u> (1 Peter 3:13-17)

Peter asks in 1 Peter 3:13, "Now who is there to hurt you if you are zealous followers of that which is good?" He said to not fear if we should have to suffer because of our faith, for in suffering we can still be blessed. Threats from others should not derail our faith in God, for we know He is in control. God will deal with all the ungodly one day.

We are to elevate Christ as our King and the ruler in our life. Peter says we should always be ready to defend our faith and explain why we are a follower of Christ. We can offer with respect the hope we have when we witness to others about what Christ means. We must be mentally strong and be prepared to withstand abuse and false accusations. Some may call you a hypocrite when you are doing your best to serve Christ. This is to be expected from some unbelievers because they feel threatened by your strong faith.

A Christ-follower never compromises or backs down from their faith. Take a firm stand for Christ and He will be by your side to give you the strength needed to withstand any attacks. Your opponent won't know how to react when you do not compromise. Your strength in Christ will be evident to those who attack your faith. Our conscience will be clear when we take a strong stand for Christ and not waiver. Always take the high road so others may aspire to be more like you.

Peter concludes in 1 Peter 3:17, "For it is better to suffer unjustly for doing right, if that should be God's will, than to suffer justly for doing wrong." Believers have faced suffering for centuries and some must suffer more than others. Verbal or physical suffering is never easy. Missionaries in foreign lands have suffered and died because they preached and taught the love of God. Their names are recorded in the Lamb's Book of Life and they will be rewarded by God according to their sacrifice.

<u>Christ's Suffering and Ours</u> (1 Peter 3:18-22) Christ suffered and died for our sins once. He died for the unrighteous, the unjust, and the guilty so He could bring us all to God. His body was executed on the cross, but He was made alive a couple of days later. We cannot imagine the pain Christ suffered because of our sins. He was the innocent Lamb of God, but He took our sins upon Himself and died in our place.

When Jesus died, His spirit went and preached to the spirits in prison. (1 Peter 3:19). These included the disobedient that rejected God during the days when Noah was building the ark. Noah preached to his neighbors for decades and they thought he was being foolish. When God shut the door to the ark and the rains started falling from heaven, it was too late for the lost to get in the ark. God cleansed the earth of all sin and all signs of sin with the great flood. Only eight people out of earth's entire population survived the flood.

Peter closes chapter 3 by talking about baptism. He said baptism is a figure of the eight people who were saved during the flood. Baptism saves us from inward concerns and fears, not by removing outward body filth, but by giving us a good and clear conscience before God. Baptism gives us inward cleansing and peace because we are imitating Jesus' death, burial, and resurrection. He died, was buried in a tomb, and arose on the third day after He was crucified. We die to sin, are buried in water at baptism, and we arise out of the water just as He came out of the tomb. He came forth with a new glorified body that will never die, and we come forth from baptism a new creation in Christ Jesus.

To turn from a life of sin and become a child of God requires a few simple but very important steps. After we hear the truth of the gospel, we realize our sinful condition and repent of our sins. We confess Jesus as the Son of God, and we are then baptized into Christ. Let's look at some scriptures that teach the connection between baptism and being saved from sin:

- Jesus commanded His apostles in Matthew 28:19 to, "Go then and make

disciples of all the nations, baptizing them into the name of the Father and of the Son and of the Holy Spirit."
- Mark 16:16, "He who believes and is baptized will be saved; but he who does not believe will be condemned."
- John 3:5, "Jesus answered him, I assure you, most solemnly I tell you, that unless a man is born of water and the Spirit, he cannot enter the kingdom of God."
- Acts 22:16, "And now, why do you delay? Rise and be baptized, and by calling upon His name, wash away your sins."

These verses speak clearly for themselves and they require no interpretation or explanation by man. There is no argument against our need to be baptized into Christ.

Jesus has now entered heaven where he sits at the right hand of God. All the angels, authorities in heaven, and powers are made sub-servient to Him. He is in God's throne room as our mediator and intercessor. He is our exalted King of kings and Lord of lords and He will reign forever and ever. Today, He awaits the arrival of all those who know Him as their Savior.

Submit in love to one another; then submit to God and let Him prove His blessings to all the faithful. James 4:7, "So be subject (*submit*) to God. Resist the devil (*stand firm against him*), and he will flee from you." When we take an active stand for Christ, we are automatically taking a pro-active stand against Satan.

Chapter Twenty-five
Serving and Suffering

It is an honor and a blessing when we can do something to help someone. The giver normally receives the greater blessing when trying to help. It may be a minor or major act of compassion, but the magnitude of the deed done is less important than the act itself. When we show someone we care for them in their time of need, the receiver of our kindness usually responds with gratitude and thankfulness. When we go the extra mile and give a sacrificial gift this increases the degree of the blessing we receive. The more we give, the more we are blessed.

Matthew 25:31-46 speaks of the end time when Jesus comes back to earth and all the holy angels will be with Him. He will sit on the throne as all nations gather before Him. He will separate the people as a shepherd separates his sheep *(the saved)* from the goats (*the lost*). The sheep will be on His right and the goats on the left. Then He will speak to the saved on the right and tell them to come and inherit the kingdom prepared for them from the time of creation. Sadly, the ones on the left who failed to accept Christ will be told to go away into eternal punishment.

Jesus shows us how important it is to help others. He said in Matthew 25:35-40, "For I was hungry and you gave Me food, I was thirsty and you gave Me something to drink, I was a stranger and you brought Me together with yourselves and welcomed and entertained and lodged Me, I was naked and you clothed Me, I was sick and you visited Me with help and ministering care, I was in prison and you came to see me." The hearers will ask Jesus when they did all these things and He will say, "Truly I tell you, in so far as you did it for one of the least of these, My brethren, you did it for Me." The least act toward someone can be blessed by God. In the final judgment, we will be judged for the things we have done in this life on earth.

Jesus addressed the unbelievers in Matthew 25:41-46. He told them they did not do any of the things the believers did for Him. They had not attended to the needs of their neighbors so they were sentenced to everlasting punishment.

Every good deed is noticed by God and is recorded in the Book of Life. It should be our goal to have our page in His book filled with good deeds. However, don't assume our good deeds alone will save us, for it is only in Christ Jesus that we find salvation. When we accept Him, it is natural to want to help others. We will want to serve Christ and this automatically leads us to serve others. Our good deeds, therefore, are simply the end result of our personal relationship with Christ.

There are three major points in 1 Peter 4. We must 1) separate from sin, 2) serve God for His glory, and 3) be willing to suffer for God's glory.

Separate from Sin (1 Peter 4:1-6)

Christ came to change the vilest, alienated sinner into His forgiven child. Every person has a past where we would like to go back and make amends for wrongs committed. No matter what we have done wrong in the past, God sent His Son, Jesus, to make all things right. We are limited in what we can do to try to rebuild the bridges of the past. If we have offended or abused someone, we should seek their forgiveness, but we cannot undo the act itself. We have the assurance Christ will forgive when we repent.

We must separate ourselves from sin to fully serve Christ. Ties with Satan are severed so we can have a close relationship with Christ. All of us have sinned and fallen short of God's expectations according to Romans 3:23. Therefore, we need to change from doing wrongful acts and do the will of God. It is time to treat others as we want to be treated.

Peter lists several things that may not apply to everyone. He lists shameless living, wantonness (*extreme thoughtlessness or loose morals*), lustful desires, drunkenness, reveling, drinking bouts, and abominable lawless idolatries. We may be able to claim innocence on some of these specific sins, but Peter's list is not all inclusive as he does not list every conceivable sin. There may be other deficiencies or sins that we have committed that Peter did not list.

Whatever our prevailing sin may be, we must face it and deal with it if we want to make corrections and amend impaired relationships. We can ignore our past wrongs, but we will have more peace of mind if we make an admission and address past problems. We must confront the individual(s) involved if we have wronged someone. Above all else, we must bring all sin to Jesus to seek and receive His forgiveness.

We are to be willing to suffer as Christ did rather than fail to please God. When we are willing to suffer for the sake of God, we have elected to stop pleasing the world so we can please God. We no longer live to satisfy personal desires, but we live to please God. This means cancelling evil relationships that draw us away from God. The friends we keep are a huge influence on our life style and actions. It is desirable, of course, to try and win our friends to Christ, but if they refuse, we are told to separate from them for our own good.

When we separate from past friends because of their evil lifestyle, they will think you are an oddball. You have decided to no longer run with the crowd who is on a road of self-destruction. They may not realize but God's Judgment Day is coming and every person must give an account of the deeds they have done on earth. We should not be concerned about man's judgment because it is God's judgment that will decide our future eternal fate or reward.

<u>Serving for God's Glory</u> (1 Peter 4:7-11)

The end-time is near, so we need to be diligent in our prayer life. We should be self-restrained against evil, sound minded, and alert. Jesus told us He will come back like a thief in the night. This calls for sound minds and patient prayers. He is coming to rapture His church and take us home to be with Him. After He raptures the church, He will later come to resurrect the unsaved to condemnation and judgment. We must be vigilant and eagerly watch for His coming.

While we await His coming, we are to have an intense and sincere love for other people. A strong love can overcome the sins of the past.

The power of love is greater than the power of past wrongs if the involved parties agree to reconciliation. Proverbs 10:12 says, "Hatred stirs up contentions, but love covers all transgressions." It is up to each individual to decide to pursue love or let past wrongs go unattended like a festered sore.

Christians are to be hospitable toward friends and strangers. We are to practice hospitality with fellow believers. This strengthens relationships and encourages unselfish teamwork within the church. We are to extend hospitality to strangers, unknown guests, foreigners, the poor, and all other believers who honor us with their presence. We should share friendship freely and without grudge to those who visit our church family. They take their time to visit and we are to show our appreciation through a warm welcome. We should never judge their past, for we all have a past; but welcome them with open arms. They need Christ just as much as we. When we are hospitable, we become an ambassador for the Lord.

Every person can contribute to the service of Christ. Each of us may have a different gift that can be used in His work.

Your gift is a precious divine endowment. We are to use our gifts to the good of God's kingdom. The gifts you possess are granted by the grace of God, so use them to please and bring glory to His name.

Whatever we say or do, we should act according to God's will. God gives us the mental capacity to speak in a manner that befits Him. We are to serve Him fully so we bring glory to Him. Our kingdom work is not about self, but rather about our Lord who sacrificed His life in our stead. We give Him glory for all He has done for us. We serve God so we can also serve others. God's grace, mercy, and compassion will be seen by others as you carry out deeds of kindness.

Why does God allow us to suffer after we commit our lives to Him? A part of the answer is found in 2 Timothy 2:12 that says, "If we endure, we shall also reign with Him. If we deny and disown and reject Him, He will also deny and disown and reject us."

Suffering for God's Glory (1 Peter 4:12-18)
Sometimes we must suffer when we serve God. Suffering is a part of God's plan for our life as it strengthens our dependence on Him. The heroes of faith mentioned in Hebrews 11 all served God faithfully, but they also suffered extremely. They testified of God's goodness with zeal and commitment, but they suffered for His sake. God has framed our destiny and He is honored to be our Sovereign God. Without faith, it is impossible

to please God (Hebrews 11:6). Our service to God is a walk of faith as we serve in faith the One we have yet to see.

God's call may not always make sense at the moment. He told Abraham to move with his wife Sarah to an undisclosed location. Through faith Abraham believed God would direct his paths to the place He intended. God gave Abraham and Sarah the physical strength for their journey. He even allowed Sarah to conceive after she had passed her child-bearing years.

Abraham was physically as good as dead as an old man when Sarah conceived. Abraham became the father of the Jewish nation and his descendants were numerous like the sand on the shore and the stars in the heavens. From a human perspective, none of this made sense when God called Abraham, but he obeyed God's call. Abraham's faith was rewarded just as God had promised.

In 1 Peter 4:12, we are told to not be amazed or bewildered at the severe trials we face to test the quality of our faith. We may feel something foreign or strange is happening in our life. There may not be an explanation for what you face when serving Christ but keep the faith. If we are in God's will, He eventually will reveal His will to us just as He did with Abraham. We walk by faith, not by sight; so just keep working for the Lord even when the end is not in view. One day, we will be able to rejoice when we see God's will revealed. Then we will know what God had in mind from the outset.

You will have achieved something significant for the Lord because you persevered through a strong faith. Isaiah 11:2 says that God may be blasphemed by others, but He is glorified through our faithful service. The spirit of God rests upon every weary worker and He provides strength so we can serve Him each day.

If we suffer as a Christian because of our allegiance to God, we should never be ashamed. Serving God even in the worst of circumstances is a privilege. We want to honor God and bring glory to His name through our meager service for Him. We thank God we are worthy to suffer for His name.

God's judgment starts with His children and then extends to the unbelievers.

If we feel God's judgment is harsh for His children, the question is how severe will His judgment be for those who have refused to accept His gift of salvation through His Son Jesus? If the righteous are barely saved, the fate of the unsaved is not good. Proverbs 11:31 warns, "The mouths of the righteous bring forth skillful and godly wisdom, but the perverse tongue shall be cut down (*like a barren and rotten tree*)."

When we suffer for Christ's sake according to God's will, we have committed our souls like a deposit to God who created us. He will never fail in His love and compassion for His children. He reigns supreme over the just and the unjust. Keep on keeping on.

Chapter Twenty-six
Shepherd of the Flock

After Jesus was resurrected by God, the Lord promoted His disciples (*learners*) and made them apostles (*the sent*). Jesus sent them into Asia Minor to teach and preach about repentance, confession, and baptism. As a part of their ministry, they would establish New Testament churches so church families could be formed. The churches needed organization and structure to operate smoothly and meet the needs of the people.

Jesus is the head of the church that has authority in the world. The voice of the church in our present society is still heard in places of power. We may feel the church is weakened by all the evil that surrounds us, but the history of the church is that it thrives in times of crisis. Conservative politicians look to the church as a large voting block that can sway an election in their favor.

The Apostle Paul wrote to Titus, "For this reason I left you (*behind*) in Crete, that you might set right what was defective and finish what was left undone, and that you might appoint elders and set them over the churches (*assemblies*) in every city as I directed you." (Titus 1:5) Christ is the Chief

Shepherd of the church but elders serve as His deputies in the local church.

The fifth chapter of first Peter is a letter of instructions to the elders in the church. Peter was an elder so he could write with authority and from his personal experiences. He had seen the good and the bad that happens in churches. Churches are made up of imperfect human beings; therefore, things don't always go as they should. God gave Peter the words to instruct elders both then and now.

Peter was not a perfect man, as he had challenges and problems like anyone else. God can use imperfect men who are willing to be led by the Holy Spirit in His church.

At times, it seemed Peter had a split personality. He could be impulsive or tender-hearted; he could be presumptuous and make assumptions and then make strong confessions of who Jesus was; he could be selfish or sacrificing; and he could deny Christ like a coward or be bold and courageous like he was when he preached to Jesus' enemies in Acts 2 on the Day of Pentecost.

God can take ordinary people with their flaws and weaknesses and use them in a mighty way to spread the gospel if their hearts are right. Today, God calls men as elders in the church who are not perfect but are committed to doing His will. When we place our faith in God and ask Him to use us as He sees fit, amazing things can happen in our life and in the life of the church. We get out of the way so God can have His way.

Peter issued a warning and some advice to the elders. He said he was an eyewitness to the suffering of Christ. He considered it an honor and privilege to serve God. The elders are overseers who are to guard and guide the local church willingly.

Elders don't coerce or goad people to do things a certain way, but they uplift others and teach out of love for Christ and His church. Elders don't lord over the church like a dictator but are to be examples of how to live and function as a Christian. Love is to always prevail over arrogance and discord.

1 Timothy chapter three gives the qualifications of an elder. An elder is to be a man who is the husband of one wife and rules his house well. He needs to have the desire to accept the responsibilities of the eldership so he can be committed to the work.

The office of an elder should never be an ego trip as the work of the Lord is a serious calling from God. He must exercise self-control and demonstrate good sense and patience. He must be dignified and live a life above reproach. Elders show love and are friendly to all who enter the church.

An elder is not a wine drinker nor is he combative; he is gentle and considerate, not quarrelsome but forbearing and peaceable. He is not a lover of money as the love of money is the root of all evil. Elders need to be experienced church workers, not a new convert, for an inexperienced person can easily buckle during a controversy. We should never let pride stand in the way of dedicated service. The elder needs a clean reputation so others cannot cast blame and bring reproach on the Lord's name. This is quite a job description and only a few men qualify for the position.

The church members should honor the elders for the responsibility they carry. Elders are the guardians and gate keepers to keep out false teaching or other things that might degrade or tarnish the witness of the church. Elders who serve faithfully according to God's will have a special reward in heaven. 1 Peter 5:4 says when Christ comes back, the elders who have served well will win the conqueror's crown of glory that won't fade away.

<u>Submission to God</u> (1 Peter 5:5-11)

The younger men and ministers are subject to the elders and are to give them due respect. They are to listen to the elder's advice and give heed to their counsel. The elders are to serve with humility as their office is of God. Elders must also be good hearers when younger men or the minister gives them input. Church leaders become a cohesive team when there is openness and respect. God expects elders to set their selfish pride and arrogance aside so they can serve effectively.

God will give grace to humble elders and give insight on tough decisions that will benefit His church. Elders humble themselves in this life so God can exalt them later.

What Peter says in 1 Peter 5:7 can apply to both elders and every believer. He wrote, "Casting the whole of your care on Him, for He cares for you." We can bring our anxieties, worries, and concerns to Christ because He cares for us with affection and love. This single verse can bring comfort, peace, and reassurance in every problem we encounter as a child of God. His arms are open to our prayers of concern for our families, the lost, and others who need a special touch from heaven.

The elders are to be on guard as the devil and his angels roam our communities and even churches seeking whom they can devour and destroy spiritually. Satan will rob us of our close relationship with Christ if we give him a foothold in our life. He is like a hungry and fierce lion that is prowling for prey. God is good all the time but the devil is evil all the time. We are warned to keep our guard up against Satan at all times. They are instructed to resist the devil and take a firm stand against him. Elders are to demonstrate strength and tenacity for the Lord as an example for others to follow.

Elders must have a strong faith so they can be an immovable force against the enemy as they serve Christ and resist Satan with a determination to win. Because of this warfare against Satan, elders may suffer for the sake of Christ. Suffering is appointed by God for His children around the world.

<u>Saints Exalted</u>

After we suffer for Christ a little while on earth, we can spend eternity with Him worry-free. Satan will be thrown into the lake of fire where he will be separated from God and His children forever. God will call all His children home where we will dwell with Him eternally.

He will make us what we ought to be and settle us for eternity. God is due all the honor and glory we can give Him for what He has in store for every believer. He has dominion and power over all of heaven and earth. We will see the complete evidence of His power when we meet Him face-to-face for the first time.

At creation, God set everything in motion for the entire universe. All the planets, stars, seasons, and time were created by God when He made night and day. He placed the sun and moon in their orbits to light the earth each day and night. The moon is God's night light for mankind and the animal kingdom. God keeps the entire creation functioning as He sustains it. Consider what would happen if God removed His powerful hand from His creation. The planets would stray from their orbits and seasons and time would be totally disrupted. It is through God's power that His creation still works today just as it did when He first made everything.

God has a plan in mind for His saints and His plan will never fade. The saints will be exalted by God when we arrive in our new heavenly home. Matthew 19:28 promises the children of God will sit on the twelve thrones that surround God's throne, and we will judge the twelve tribes of Israel.

Luke 19:17 says because we were faithful in a little, we will have authority over ten cities. Revelation 3:21 tells us that overcomers will be allowed to sit with Jesus on His throne. Christ has overcome and so have we. God has good things in store for His children that we cannot begin to imagine. Our first challenge is to be an overcomer on earth.

James 4:10 says we are to humble ourselves in the presence of the Lord, and He will exalt us. We are insignificant in His presence but He will lift us up and make us significant.

What a transformation we can expect when we trade in our earthly body that is diseased and weak for a glorified body that will be just like Jesus' new body. Our glorified bodies will be fit to dwell with Jesus for eternity and they will never get sick or die.

Divine Grace

We will close our study of first Peter by looking at God's grace that He extends to each of us. Grace is God's favor that we do not deserve. His grace is available to every unbeliever who needs salvation, and all the redeemed for victorious living. God's grace empowers us for service and it enables us to lead simple but dedicated lives. We are to extend grace (*undeserved favor*) to others the same way Jesus did.

1 Corinthians 3:10 tells us God has bestowed or endowed us with His grace. God is like a skilled architect and master builder. The Apostles Peter and Paul laid the foundation but others would follow who would continue the spiritual building of God. Our foundation

is Jesus Christ. He gives grace to every worker in His kingdom and this gift gives us purpose and determination for loyal and faithful service.

What an honor to be able to continue the work of great men like Paul, Peter, James, and John. They started the work of spreading the gospel and we have the privilege to continue telling the good news of a risen Savior to the world. Others will follow our footsteps and continue to spread the gospel if the Lord does not come back first.

God's grace is necessary for salvation. 1 Corinthians 15:11 says we are saved through the grace of our Lord Jesus. In Ephesians 2:5, Paul wrote, "Even when we were dead by our shortcomings and trespasses, He made us alive together in fellowship and in union with Christ; it is by grace that you are saved."

Jesus' sacrifice on Calvary and God's grace make salvation possible for all who will believe. Because of His grace, we are justified and made right in the sight of God. We become heirs because of the hope of eternal life (Titus 5:7).

Peter preached and wrote about the Lord Jesus Christ who came to earth to enable us to find salvation. In so doing, we gain heaven and shun an awful place of punishment.

God's amazing grace is available to all who will believe.

Chapter Twenty-seven
The Faithful

The apostle Peter wrote two letters (*epistles*). We are uncertain when he wrote his first letter, but Bible scholars feel he wrote Second Peter around A.D. 64-70. The first letter had two main themes: 1) to encourage and strengthen believers who had scattered to several surrounding countries and 2) to feed the flock as Jesus instructed them. The second epistle was written as a warning to believers of the dangerous and seductive work of false teachers. Peter encourages us to grow in the grace of God so we can discern false teachers and close our ears to them. Second Peter is intended for all Christians worldwide.

The only way we can understand and know when a false teacher is in our midst is to be grounded in the scriptures. Paul said in 2 Timothy 2:15 to study the scriptures to show ourselves approved by God. We must know the truth so we can identify a lie spoken by a false teacher. The elders in the church are to guard the church family from false teachers and silence them should they appear in our worship services, small groups, or Sunday school.

A false teacher is an advocate of the devil who seeks to divide and weaken the church. It is Satan's desire to supplant false teachers in place of grounded Bible teachers. The church leadership has the accountability to vet every teacher before allowing them to teach. Teachers who are true to the Word of God have no problem answering the elder's questions about their faith and beliefs. Things can get out-of-hand quickly when a false teacher is allowed to teach. False teaching is a serious offense against God and brings great harm to the church.

A false teacher is like the false prophets mentioned in the book of Revelation. The apostle John wrote in Revelation 20:10 that the devil, the beast (*antichrist*), and the false prophets will all be cast into the lake of fire and brimstone where they will be tormented forever and ever.

<u>Precious Promises</u> (2 Peter 1:1-4)

Peter was appointed by Jesus to be an apostle, or special messenger, to those who wanted to share in his faith. Peter was commissioned to preach to the Jews who had killed Jesus. The Day of Pentecost was one of the important feasts the Jews celebrated each year. Pentecost was celebrated fifty days after the Passover celebration. June was the third month in the Jewish calendar and

June 6 was the designated date for the Feast of Pentecost at the end of the wheat harvest. The feast commemorated the giving of the Law by God to Moses. Pentecost and the other annual feast days were all very important to the Jewish people.

In Acts 2, Peter stood to preach to the Jews on the Day of Pentecost. He told them they had killed their Messiah who arose on the third day after His crucifixion just as He promised. They were aware Jesus had come forth from death and they were disturbed over what they had done. They listened to Peter preach and then asked, "What shall we do?" Peter told them in Acts 2:38, "Repent and be baptized, every one of you, in the name of Jesus Christ for the forgiveness and release from your sins; and you shall receive the gift of the Holy Spirit." About 3,000 people responded to Peter's message and were baptized that same day.

When we understand and embrace the fact of Jesus' death, burial, resurrection, and ascension, then we can appreciate more fully what Peter says in 2 Peter 2-4. He pronounces a blessing on their behalf by directing their attention to God's grace and peace that he wanted to be upon them. Peter wanted them to enjoy spiritual prosperity, and freedom from fears, passions, and moral conflicts. He wanted God's grace to multiply as they personally developed a deeper knowledge of God and His Son Jesus.

God has given His children all we need to have a strong relationship with Him and lead a godly life. We want to learn more about God and His plan so He will continue to bless us with spiritual strength. We can become strong warriors for God as we wage war against Satan when we are armed with God's truth. Knowing our Commander-in-Chief's desires enables us to be an excellent soldier who can withstand the rigors of war with Satan.

Our personal battles and struggles may differ from someone else's, but we are all called to battle for what is right and acceptable to God. He gives us His precious promises that will help us stay focused on our mission. His promises help us understand and escape the moral decay we see in our community. Morals have sunk to a low point as people openly commit sins that smell like rotten food to God, for He abhors all sin. Christians share in God's divine promises that He can and will lead us through this world to a much better life in eternity. We must stay in the battle for what is right.

Growing in Faith (2 Peter 1:5-11)

It has been said we can know a tree by the fruit it bears. The same is true for the believer and unbeliever. A person is easily defined spiritually by their actions. An evil person will espouse hatred, jealousy, pride, greed, etc., while a godly person will bear the fruits of the Spirit including love, peace, kindness, etc.

Peter lists some of the fruits the child of God should bear in 2 Peter 1:5-7. We should be diligent and attentive to God's divine promises. We will make a serious effort to exercise our faith that helps develop spiritual energy to do God's work. We strive to learn more about God and His will. The result will be self-control, patience, endurance, steadfastness, godliness, brotherly love, and Christian love. When a person practices these godly gifts that come by knowing Him, then others can also be blessed.

Striving to bear fruit for the Lord is a constant process each day. These are not things we exhibit only on Sunday, but they become interwoven traits in our daily life. When we are busy bearing fruit for the Lord, there is no time for idleness or being unfruitful. We must be engaged and pro-active for the Lord if we are to do our utmost for Him.

The idle person who has professed Christ is spiritually blind and short-sighted to his/her God-given abilities. They only see what is at hand as they have no vision for the future God has promised. The individual who once believed but has fallen away, is blind to the fact he was once cleansed from his old sins and made a new person in Christ at baptism. Peter warns us to be eager and make sure to be more steadfast to our calling. This will enable us to not stumble or fall in our walk with God. He is waiting to welcome us into the eternal kingdom of our Lord. This is a promise from God.

<u>Peter's Approaching Death</u> (2 Peter 1:12-15)
The most certain thing about life is the uncertainty of it. Life is fragile and death is sure. Death can come to the young or the old with or without warning, but we know it is certain and sure.

Peter's desire was to sound a warning to hold fast to the things they already knew. Peter did not have to remind them of the rich promises of God or the fruits they needed to bear for Him. They already knew the truth about the things God expects.

Peter referred to his earthly body in other Bible translations as a tent. A tent is easily set-up, torn down, and moved to another location. A tent is temporary and not permanent. Nomads who live in tents in the desert understand these things as they move from one area to another with their sheep.

Peter said while he was in his body that he called a tent, that it would always be his intention to remind Christians of the things Christ has given us so we can do His work. He wanted to stir up their memory so they would never forget God's goodness.

Jesus had obviously revealed to Peter that his death would be rapid in the near future. In 2 Peter 1:14, Peter said, "Since I know that the laying aside of this body of mine will come speedily, as our Lord Jesus Christ made clear to me." His desire was that his fellow-believers would never forget after his death what he told them. Peter hoped the truth of the gospel he shared would be his legacy after he died. He wanted them to have instant recall of his teachings.

<u>The Word</u> (2 Peter 1:16-21)

Peter was not relaying a fairy tale to them when he taught the things of God. He did not offer them man's theory, but he plainly gave them the truth of the gospel. He was an eyewitness about the power of God and he fully believed in the coming of our Lord. He had seen Jesus' power of miracles and His authority that came from God. Jesus is grand, majestic, and sovereign and Peter had witnessed it all as he labored with Christ throughout His ministry.

Peter was with Christ one day on the Mount of Transfiguration (Luke 9:28-35). Jesus took Peter, James, and John with him up on a mountain to pray. As Jesus prayed, the appearance of His face changed and His robe changed to glistening white. Moses and Elijah appeared from heaven in their glorious bodies and talked to Jesus about His upcoming death in Jerusalem. Jesus' three disciples went into a deep sleep. When they awoke, they saw Jesus, Moses, and Elijah in all their brilliant glory.

As Moses and Elijah were leaving, Peter suggested to Jesus it would be good if they built three huts or booths for Jesus, Moses, and Elijah. A cloud moved in and the three disciples were overcome with fear as Moses and Elijah disappeared in the cloud. A loud voice came out of the cloud and told Peter, "This is My Son, My Chosen One, or My Beloved, listen to and yield to and obey Him!" They had seen a glimpse of the glory of heaven and received God's direct command to listen and obey His Son.

Peter referred to this voice of God from the cloud in 2 Peter 1:17. He said God told the disciples that day, "This is My beloved Son in Whom I am well pleased and delight." Peter testified to seeing this glorious sight to those who listened. He also told them he had the prophetic word that made the truth of Christ even more firm. He asked them to pay close attention to Christ who was a lamp shining in darkness. He said the darkness will flee when the Morning Star (*Jesus*) becomes real to them.

He reminded them that no prophecy came from man, but from God. Prophets were God's mouthpieces in Old Testament times to relay His messages and warnings to kings and nations. Peter gave God full credit for being behind what these men of old boldly said.

Chapter Twenty-eight
Deceptive Teachers

When someone speaks the truth, they speak facts, not fiction. Believers in the truth place a high value on speaking factually on all subjects. Liars and all other unforgiven sinners are promised the lake of fire where they will be cast along with Satan, the antichrist, and false prophets.

When some are untruthful, they say they told a fib and not a lie. A fib is what some consider as a little less damning than an outright lie. They may even say a fib is a casual or mild lie. If there is a line or a difference between a fib and a lie, it is a very fine and almost invisible line. A fib or a lie is not the truth. The church unfortunately is not immune to liars.

Peter's warning in 2 Peter 2 expresses his obvious concern about false teachers in the church. A false teacher is someone under the control of Satan whether it is in church or elsewhere. They are a serious danger as they paint a false picture and expect people to accept what they say as truth. A false teacher may spread enough misinformation over time that they don't even know the truth any longer. Satan feeds them his lies and deceit on a regular basis and they in turn convey the same information to others. The real danger is if we keep hearing a lie repeatedly, it can eventually be accepted as truth.

<u>False Teachers</u> (2 Peter 2:1-11)

There were false prophets in the Old Testament which was long before Christ's or Peter's births. The prophet Jeremiah wrote his book of prophecy in 627 B.C.

God warned the people in Jeremiah 23.16, "Thus says the Lord of hosts: Do not listen to the words of the (*false*) prophets who prophesy to you. They teach you vanity (*emptiness, falsity, and futility*) and fill you with vain hopes; they speak a vision of their own minds and not from the mouth of the Lord." The problem of false teachers preceded Christ's birth for centuries. What they taught were man's manufactured thoughts with the help of Satan.

The devil's primary mode of operation is deceit and lies. He lied three times when Jesus was in the wilderness for forty days after He was baptized (Luke 4:2-13). He tempted Christ just as he tempts us. Jesus was tempted with lust of the eyes, the lust of the flesh, and the pride of life. Jesus firmly resisted the temptations by refusing Satan's worldly honor. The devil hates the Bible for it is God's truth, and Satan cannot stand the truth. Here is how Jesus responded to Satan's temptations:

- "It is written, Man shall not live and be sustained by bread alone but by every word and expression of God." (Luke 4:4)
- "Get behind Me, Satan! It is written, you shall do homage to worship the Lord your God, and Him only shall you serve." (Deuteronomy 6:13 and Luke 4:8)
- "You shall not tempt the Lord your God." (Deuteronomy 6:16 and Luke 4:12)

After Christ resisted Satan on each lie and temptation, he left Jesus alone.

A lie is a very damaging action, but in most cases a lie will eventually come to light. There is no justification for a lie. The pain of the truth is not nearly as great as the disappointment of a lie. We can usually deal with the temporary pain of the truth much easier than the long-term damage of a lie.
2 Peter 2:1 says the false prophets lied to the people many years previously, the same as there were false teachers in Peter's day.

Satan was at work in the Old Testament, the New Testament, and he is still on duty today. False prophets subtly taught untrue doctrines that eventually brought destruction. They even denied and disowned Jesus who bought them with the price of His blood. Many people unfortunately followed the immoral ways of the false teachers, thereby God's true Way (*Jesus*) is maligned and defamed.

Lust and greed are used to draw people into Satan's trap as the false teachers speak cunning words. False teachers have always been active as they have neither been idle nor asleep.

Doom awaits false teachers according to 2 Peter 2:4. God did not spare the angels that sinned, but cast them into hell (*Hades*), to be kept there in pits of gloom till the judgment and their eternal doom. In Noah's day, God did not spare the ungodly when He brought a flood upon the earth. Only Noah and his God-fearing family survived the flood.

The cities of Sodom and Gomorrah were condemned and brought to ruin because of their sins. They were known for widespread homosexuality and other sins. God rescued Lot and his family from Sodom and Gomorrah because he was a righteous man living in a very sinful place. Lot was worn out and distressed with the wanton ways of the ungodly and lawless citizens of his city. Lot's neighbors tortured his righteous soul daily when he saw the evil that had them addicted to Satan. God then reduced the two cities to ashes, making them an example for all ungodly people.

Lot's rescue gives us hope that the Lord knows how to rescue the godly out of temptations, sin, and trials. He keeps the ungodly in safety for the Day of Judgment and doom for the unsaved.

Satan and his followers cannot anticipate a good outcome for their evil actions on earth. Some indulge in lustful passion and despise authority. They are self-willed and self-loving people and they scoff at good leaders. Holy Angels who have superior might and power do not bring a charge against them before the Lord.

We live in an evil world. It is discouraging and stressful to see the many bad things going on around us: looting, killing, stealing, abuse, abortion, human trafficking, and all sorts of other sins are a grave concern. God is letting Satan run rampant on the earth for now, but one day He will call a halt to the devil so justice can be done and God's people can find peace.

<u>Depravity of False Teachers</u> (2 Peter 2:12-17)

False teachers are depraved and corrupt. They are like beasts without any reasoning ability. They operate on instinct, not logic. They teach and rail out about things they don't understand. False teachers are ignorant when it comes to the facts. They destroy and eventually they will be destroyed. Their reward will be God's punishment as they will suffer for their wrongs. They are like a cancer on humanity that eats away at men's souls. They sit back and laugh at man's gullibility as they thrive on sin like a harlot. They target people who are unstable in their faith and lure them into their trap. They are a curse like a plague on the earth. They have strayed far from God's pathway and they love wickedness.

In Numbers 22:20-35, we are given the account of Balaam. God spoke to Balaam during the night and told him if men came to him, to not go with them. He was to do only what God told him. The next morning Balaam went with the princes of Moab before God instructed him to go.

The Lord sent an Angel to block his route. Balaam's donkey saw an Angel with a sword in his hand, but Balaam did not see him. The donkey turned and went into the field to escape. Balaam tried unsuccessfully three times to get the donkey back on the trail. He would strike the donkey each time for her disobedience. God gave the donkey a voice and she asked Balaam in Numbers 22: 28, "What have I done to you that you should strike me these three times?" The Lord opened Balaam's eyes and he finally saw the Angel standing in his way. He fell on his face and told the Angel he would go back home if that is what he wanted. The Angel told Balaam to go with the men, but only say what He told him. The donkey saved Balaam from being killed by the Angel.

False teachers have forsaken God's straight road. Balaam was rebuked when the donkey revealed the truth to him. False teachers will also be rebuked and punished according to God's plan. False teachers are like springs without water as they don't contribute anything good for God or man. Gloom and doom are reserved for them by God.

<u>Deceptions of False Teachers</u> (2 Peter 2:18-22)

The power of false teachers should never be minimized or under-estimated. They have been empowered by Satan to speak very persuasive and cunning words. They boast and lure people with their lustful desires of the flesh. They promise liberty and freedom when they themselves are slaves to their own depravity and defilement. They fall into the same trap of Satan as his followers. Satan gives the false teachers the power of persuasion, but he can also withdraw that power and the false teacher then becomes a victim to Satan.

Some people see the light and try to escape the snare of the false teacher, only to become entrapped again.

2 Peter 2:20 tells us, "For if, after they have escaped the pollutions of the world through (*the full, personal*) knowledge of our Lord and Savior Jesus Christ, they again become entangled in them and are overcome. Their last condition is worse (*for them*) than the first." They never really understood God's way of righteousness, so they were worse off by trying to return to God. Satan destroys our moral compass and tries to snare us into his trap. His power of allurement has always been strong.

The Cure for Standing against False Teachers
There is no vaccination or cure to guard against false teachers. Our best defense comes from knowing Jesus as our Savior and immersing ourselves in His Word. When we accept Christ as our Lord, we have enthroned Jesus and dethroned Satan; but that doesn't mean Satan will walk away and leave us alone. He knows our weaknesses and this is where he will try and chip away at our faith. Satan knows if lust, greed, or pride is where we are weakest.

Accepting Christ is easy, but fighting Satan takes a strong commitment to the Lord. We must turn to God for strength to fight in His army. God has sent His Holy Spirit to help us every day. He will never leave us or forsake us, so we depend on Him to help us each day.

Christ gave us a perfect example on how to deal with Satan. First, we must take a firm stand against temptation. To do that, we should tell Satan we are a child of God and we have no place for him in our life. We can also tell Satan to get behind us as we are walking with Christ as our guide. We can tell him we will not accept him back as the lord of our life as Jesus is now our Lord. Satan hates us when we bring Jesus into the conversation. Satan knows he has competition when we claim Jesus as our Lord and he knows that one day he will lose for eternity.

Perseverance is needed as Satan does not give up easily. He will keep coming back and attack us when we are alone or depressed. He knows when and where we are the most vulnerable. We cannot afford to let down our defense against Satan lest he overpowers us. Satan does not operate alone as he has an army of angels that can also attack us.

Study your Bible and pray to God often. He will strengthen and encourage you as you strive to please Him in all words and actions.

Chapter Twenty-nine
The Promise of God

There are many promises made by God and Jesus throughout the Bible. God's children rely and stand on these promises because this is what keeps us focused on the end game. This short life on earth is just a prelude to eternal life with God and His Son Jesus. Some of God's promises help us navigate this life, while other promises relate to eternity. God has either kept or will keep every promise.

A bride and groom promise their love and loyalty to each other until death. About 50% of all marriages unfortunately fail in America. It is easy for man to break a promise, but God will never break even one of His. When we buy something on credit, we promise to repay the debt as agreed upon. Most people take a debt repayment promise seriously, but some fail to pay for whatever reason. If a promise cannot be kept due to unforeseen circumstances, it is incumbent that we communicate and work out a satisfactory arrangement. Most of the time, common ground can be found if pursued. To ignore a legitimate debt doesn't make it go away.

We are all debtors to Christ for what He did for us on Calvary. God planned for Christ to become our sacrifice before creation. He foresaw how man would fall to sin and would need a way back to Him. Sin separates us from God, but Christ is our bridge back to God who has promised if we come humbly to Him in repentance, He will forgive our sins. This opens the door to eternal life with Him because He will keep His promise.

<u>The Promise of His Coming</u> (2 Peter 3:1-9)
Peter loved his fellow servants of Christ and he even called them "Beloved" in 2 Peter 3:1. He wrote this second letter to them out of love. He said both of his letters in 1 Peter and 2 Peter were written with a sincere mind on the things he wanted them to remember. The prophets made predictions many years earlier about the upcoming birth of Christ. Jesus issued commandments and instructions through His apostles and Peter wanted them to remember all these things. A good starting point for any Christian is to remember the things God has promised.

Peter warned them about scoffers or mockers who would come in the last days. He said the scoffers or pretenders walk after their own fleshly desires and they mock Christians who are walking with Christ. They will ask, "Where is the promise of His coming? For since the forefathers fell asleep, all things have continued exactly as they did from the beginning of creation" (2 Peter 3:4). They intentionally forgot how the heavens and earth came into existence at creation by God's spoken word. The people who believe in evolution leave God completely out of creation. They base their belief on science instead of accepting God's written Word about how all things were created by Him.

The earth was completely covered with water when God first created it. God spoke at creation and all things came into being. He then caused dry land to come out of the water to form the continents. God created every brook, creek, river, lake, and ocean. Without Him nothing, including man, would exist.

The same power God used at creation was used to reserve the heavens and earth for fire when He purifies them for all eternity in the end-time. The heavens and earth will melt with intense and fervent heat when God removes all signs of sin from His creation. This is His promise and He has the power and intent to do exactly what He said.

When people ask when Jesus will return, we have to say we don't know. We accept God's promise through faith that Jesus will definitely come back at God's appointed time. Jesus and the angels don't know when He will come back either. Only God knows the date when He will order Jesus to come back to rapture His church. Foolish men have tried to pinpoint the date for Jesus' return in the past, only to be embarrassed by a failed prediction.

Moses prayed a prayer to God in Psalm 90:4 where he said, "For a thousand years in your sight are but as yesterday when it is past, or as a watch in the night." A watchman in the night only stands guard for a short time. A long time for us is a short time for God. We have clocks, watches, cell phones, and computers to keep track of time, but God does not need any of these devices. He is the Father of time, as He created it.

Peter echoed Moses in 2 Peter 3:8 by saying, "Nevertheless, do not let this one fact escape you, beloved, that with the Lord one day is as a thousand years and a thousand years as one day." Jesus' ascension back to heaven after His resurrection was over 2,000 years ago for us, but it was just a couple of days ago on God's time table. We want God to move quicker than He plans in many cases, but God will move only when He is ready to execute His plan to send Jesus to rapture the church. He is not slow or tardy in keeping His promises as we might think. He is a very patient God toward mankind as He does not want one person to perish in their sins. Only God knows the best time to send Jesus back to get His church. It is His desire that every person be given the opportunity to accept Christ rather than coming sooner and seeing too many lost souls who must be cast into the lake of fire with Satan at the end.

<u>The Day of the Lord</u> (2 Peter 3:10-13)
God will decide when Jesus will come as a thief when the heavens and earth will vanish and pass away.

There will be a loud thunderous noise and the material elements of the universe will be dissolved with intense heat. The earth and everything on it will be burned up. We take pride in our houses, cars, bank accounts, etc., but one day they will all go up in flames. God promised after the great flood in Noah's day He would never destroy the earth with water again. He put a rainbow in the cloud to affirm His promise and intentions. The next purification of the earth will be by fire and intense heat when the heavens, its elements, and the earth will melt.

The question is asked on what kind of persons we ought to be in the meantime. Peter urges us to be consecrated to God with holy behavior and godly qualities. We should eagerly and earnestly await the coming of the Lord. Many long for His coming due to the problems in this life. Too many of our family and close friends have departed through death. We yearn for His coming so we can be in the perfect place with perfected people.

The first heaven and the first earth as we know them presently will be dissolved in fire and heat. There will then be a new heaven and new earth as He promised. Only those in right standing with God will be able to live eternally with God. Those whose sins have been washed away by the blood of the Lamb will live eternally with God, Christ, the prophets, the apostles, the patriarchs, the angels, and our loved ones. There will be no more separation, for there will be no more death.

We live in the confidence of His coming after we become His child. We are eager to be found by Jesus when He comes. He will look for us like a shepherd goes out to find a lost sheep that has strayed from the flock, and He will find us. His coming does not frighten us when we know our sins are forgiven. We have a hope and expectation beyond this world. In the meantime, God practices patience so more people can accept Christ. God would rather see people saved instead of being banished to outer darkness to a place of torment.

We must be careful, for some will take the scriptures and twist and distort them to mean something else. We should never try to alter God's Word or the intent of His Word. It is dangerous and deadly when we try to usurp God as we try to improve His perfect Word.

Peter realized that a person who has accepted Christ can still back slide. He warns us in 2 Peter 3:17 we should be on guard; otherwise, we can be carried away by lawless and wicked people and fall from our position with God. We must remain firm in our convictions and steadfast in our love and commitment to the Lord.

Peter closes his book with words of encouragement for every believer. He tells us to grow in the grace of God, and the knowledge of the Lord Jesus Christ. His final words give God praise by saying, "To Him (*be*) glory (*honor, majesty, and splendor*) both now and to the day of eternity. Amen

Introduction to James

Jesus' half-brother James wrote a letter to Jewish converts to Christianity who lived beyond the borders of Israel. Jews of the dispersion were scattered throughout the known world, and many of them had accepted Christ. James wanted to encourage them in their faith as he gave them specific things they should or should not do as a Christian.

James made two strong points:
- The mark of a true Christian.
- The results of a false profession of Christ as Lord.

He challenged them to have an active and strong faith by doing certain things that would strengthen their walk with the Lord. James encourages us to be fair and just with our fellow man and to treat everyone equally. He promotes a strong faith that produces good works for the Lord.

James also offers advice on the control of our tongue, pride, and boasting. Humble service is required in our daily walk with the Lord. We are to be patient and steadfast in our faith through tenacious endurance.

Chapter Thirty
Gain through Loss

Jesus' half-brother James is believed to be the author of the book of James. Mary was the mother of Jesus and James, but Joseph was not the biological father of Jesus. Mary mothered Jesus through the power of God who worked through the Holy Spirit so she could conceive and give birth to Jesus. Mary and Joseph were the biological parents of James. James, Jesus' half-brother is not the same James whom Jesus called as one of His twelve disciples.

The book of James was most likely one of the earliest New Testament books written. Jesus' half-brothers did not believe in Him until possibly after His resurrection following His crucifixion. Sometimes family members are the most difficult for us to influence to come to Christ. This was the case with Jesus' half-brothers.

James encourages and urges all believers to have a strong and active faith. Such a faith produces positive changes in a person's words and actions. A strong faith will be reflected in our behavior and lifestyle. It is easy to profess our faith, but much more difficult to show our faith to others through compassionate actions. When we show love and compassion, we are blessed.

<u>Profit from Trials</u> (James 1:1-8)

James starts his book by saying he was a servant of God and the Lord. His letter is directed to the Jews who had scattered from Israel into different parts of the known world. This is referred to as the dispersion of the Jews.

In Acts 2, Peter was privileged to preach to the Jews of the dispersion on the Day of Pentecost. They had met to hear Peter preach and the Holy Spirit fell on the disciples and gave them the ability to speak fifteen different languages/dialects.

The Jews in Peter's audience came to Jerusalem from throughout the whole region from countries with modern names of Egypt, Iran, Iraq, Turkey, Rome, Arabia, Crete, and Israel. The Holy Spirit fell on the disciples so they could speak in all these languages and dialects. The disciples were ordinary men who had not had foreign language training. The power of the Holy Spirit is amazing when we yield our lives to Christ.

There are other instances in the New Testament where the Holy Spirit came in a very real and strong manner to people. The Holy Spirit is the third person in the Trinity or Godhead. The Trinity is made up of God the Father, Jesus His Son, and the Holy Spirit. The Holy Spirit is a conduit of God's power that flows into our lives. In the Old Testament, God spoke through prophets to deliver His message. In the New Testament, He spoke through the apostles. Today He speaks to us through the Holy Spirit.

In Luke 1:13-17, an angel visited Zachariah and told him his wife, Elizabeth, would bear a son and they would call his name John (*the Baptist*). Zachariah and Elizabeth were both well beyond child-bearing age, but God demonstrated His power by allowing the humanly impossible to occur. The angel told Zachariah that John would be controlled by the Holy Spirit even while he was in his mother's womb. John the Baptist grew up and became a very powerful man with the help of the Spirit as he foretold the coming of the Messiah. John the Baptist was similar to the Old Testament prophets who could foretell future events because of God's messages to them.

Jesus was filled and controlled by the Holy Spirit. John the Baptist baptized Jesus in the Jordan River in Luke 3:22. The Holy Spirit descended upon Jesus in bodily form like a dove, and a voice from heaven said, "You are My Son, My Beloved! In You I am well pleased and find delight!" From the day of His baptism to the time of His resurrection the Holy Spirit dwelt in Jesus. Today, that same Holy Spirit dwells in the hearts of all believers.

In Luke 4:1-2, Jesus was led by the Holy Spirit immediately after He was baptized into the wilderness for forty days. He fasted and prayed, and Satan tempted Him. Jesus was physically hungry during His forty-day test, but at the end, the angels came and ministered to Him. Jesus was drained physically but filled spiritually. Sometimes we don't have answers to serious problems. We may even feel spiritual hunger and a gap in our relationship with God, but this is when the Holy Spirit can minister to us with spiritual food and strength.

It didn't take Satan long to try and take control of Jesus after He arrived in the desolate and lonely place. Through his deception, Satan offered worldly honor to Jesus. Satan also tries to destroy our faith when we feel alone with no one to come to our aid. The Holy Spirit gives us the power to withstand the evil in our world.

In Acts 13:6-12, we find the Apostle Paul, John Mark, and Barnabas in Cyprus to preach. Before they departed for Cyprus, they fasted and prayed and the Holy Spirit fell on them. The Holy Spirit gave them instructions to go to Cyprus. In Cyprus, there was a magician called a sorcerer and false prophet named Bar-Jesus (*Elymas*) who was a friend of the proconsul, Sergius Paulus. A proconsul was a Roman official who was a deputy consul in a local province. Sergius Paulus wanted to meet with the missionaries so he could hear the Word of God concerning salvation and the kingdom of God that we obtain through Jesus Christ.

Elymas opposed Paul and wanted to keep Sergius Paulus from accepting Christ. Paul, who was filled with and controlled by the Holy Spirit, looked Elymas in the eye and called him the son of the devil. Paul told Elymas he would go blind for a period of time and he did. Elymas had to depend on others to lead him around because he could not even see the sun. When Sergius Paulus saw the power of God working through the Holy Spirit and Paul, he accepted Christ.

The power of the Holy Spirit is amazing because God's power is unlimited. The Holy Spirit receives His power directly from God. James 1:2-3 tells us to count it joy when we are faced with trials or are tempted. Trials and temptations come to us all, and at times they overwhelm us. We may be tempted to think God is punishing us, but this is not the case. We are instructed to face trials and temptations with joy. Just as Jesus was tempted by Satan, our faith is also tested through trials and temptations. The testing of our faith brings endurance, steadfastness, and patience when we let the Holy Spirit empower us to withstand Satan as the Apostle Paul did.

Paul wrote in 2 Corinthians 12:10, "So for the sake of Christ, I am well pleased and take pleasure in infirmities, insults, hardships, persecutions, perplexities, and distresses; for when I am weak (*in human strength*), then am I strong (*in divine strength*)." The Holy Spirit comes to us when we are drained of human strength and fills our emptiness with God's spiritual strength. His strength is our spiritual food that will nourish our souls so we can strive even more diligently to do His work. We are called to believe in Christ and to also suffer for His sake. We are to suffer without self-pity and complaining because we sometimes suffer due to our close relationship with Christ.

In times of trouble, we may not know which way to turn. James 1:5 says that if we lack wisdom, we should ask God and He will give it liberally. God does not find fault when we ask Him for wisdom. He already knows our human frailty and limited wisdom. He is all-wise and can give us wisdom through His

Word and the Holy Spirit. When we ask God for wisdom, we must do so in faith believing and without doubting God's ability to answer our prayer.

A weak faith causes doubt, and this can lead us to the point of going whichever way the wind blows instead of walking by faith with God. A doubter knows God won't hear and answer. A double-minded person is unstable and uncertain about all things spiritual.

<u>The Rich and the Poor</u>   (James 1:9-11)

God created the rich and the poor. A person who owns little of this world's goods can be amazingly rich in faith. Poor people living in third world countries live in huts with no windows, doors, or floors. They are the poorest of the poor, but many of them are the most joyful and appreciative people on earth. Possessions and nice houses do not bring joy and happiness. These blessings come from God who is rich in grace and mercy. True richness is found in being called a child of God and a joint heir with Christ of all God's riches.

Conversely, a rich person may know about God but they may not know Him. The natural tendency is to rely on our accumulation of wealth and knowledge instead of God to meet our daily and future needs. A rich person can easily feel independent without much need for God. Riches can be a threat to our faith if we don't manage them according to God's plan. Our riches can be a blessing, or they can be a detriment to our walk with God. Wealth can be a major distraction in serving God if we don't give Him first place in our life. Many years ago a wealthy businessman gave God the credit for his success. He started his business with one retail store. From this humble beginning, his business empire grew into a nationwide chain of department stores. He became very wealthy, but he never forgot it was God who provided and enabled his success. It is said the man tithed 90% of his income so he could give back to God. This man did not let his riches lead him down the wrong path. A rich person can bring many blessings to others if he is willing to share what God has freely given.

The independent rich person, who does not regard God for his blessing, is subject to downfall. James 1:10 says the rich person ought to give God glory because he can be humbled and pass away like the grass fades and withers. Life is short, fragile, and uncertain for the rich and the poor.

In Luke 12:15, Jesus said a man's life does not consist in and is not derived from possessing excessive abundance that exceeds his needs. He spoke a parable about a farmer whose rich fertile land yielded a bountiful crop. He had no place to store the excess harvest. The farmer said, "I will do this: I will pull down my storehouses and build larger ones, and there I will store all my grain and all my goods." In this one sentence, the rich and blessed farmer referred to himself six times. He did not thank God once for blessing him so abundantly. He went on to say he now had enough assets to last for many years, so he told himself to take it easy, eat, drink, and enjoy himself fully.

But God said to the man, "You fool! This very night, they (*God's angels*) will demand your soul of you; and all the things that you have prepared, whose will they be?" Our possessions will mean little when we face an earthly death. People won't praise us about our wealth, for it is no longer of any benefit. But if we have been a compassionate and caring person, these are the things that will be remembered. Our faith in God is the most important thing we can possess.

Loving God When Tried (James 1:12-18)

James 1:12 says, "Blessed (*happy, to be envied*) is the man who is patient under trial and stands up under temptation, for when he has stood the test and been approved, he will receive the crown of life (*victor's crown*) which God has promised to those who love Him."

A child of God must be prepared to suffer with dignity as we work our way through trials and temptations as a victor, not a victim. God has promised the overcomers a victor's crown of life. It takes a strong faith to be able to endure trials and tribulations as a strong and patient person. The Holy Spirit is our Helper in all situations.

A man who lost his spouse, daughter, and granddaughter said he never questioned or blamed God for his losses. Instead, he suffered quietly without complaining. This is the mark of a true Christian whose faith is grounded in the Lord. We may not fully understand God's plan, but we accept what comes our way as God's will. We are to keep our faith and cling to God who is our Anchor during the storm.

God tempts no man, for He is not tempted by evil. He is pure, righteous, and all-powerful. We are tempted when we let our guard down and are driven by our desires. Satan entices us to sin, just as he did with Eve when he convinced her she should listen to him instead of God. Eve ate the forbidden fruit God told her plainly not to eat. The day Eve and then Adam ate the fruit, mankind came under God's curse of pain and death.

Mankind will continue to live under the curse of pain and death until Jesus makes all things new at the Last Day.

When we yield to Satan and intentionally commit sin, our selfish desire has conceived and brought forth sin. When sin is fully mature, it brings forth death. Romans 6:23 says, "For the wages which sin pays is death, but the free gift of God is eternal life through Jesus Christ our Lord." We can live a life of sin and be rewarded with a second death, or we can live for Christ and receive eternal life.

James reminds us that every good and perfect gift comes from God. It is of His own free will that He gave us a Savior. As His child, we are examples of all His creation. He made us higher than the animals so we are His first fruit and shepherds to all the animal kingdom.

We are to be quick to hear and slow to speak or show wrath. Taking offense or showing anger is not according to God's plan for our life. There are times when we can rightly show anger when it involves Satan and his deceit and lies. He is out to destroy our faith and it is acceptable as one of God's soldiers to go to war with Satan. He will destroy relationships and divide families and churches if we are not constantly on guard.

God's Action Plan (James 1:21-27)

There are proactive things God expects us to do in our daily walk with Him. We are to be humble and ready to take the actions needed to fully serve Him. God tells us to clean our spiritual house and get rid of anything that is unclean or wicked. We need to unclutter our spiritual life just as we would clean our house. We are to accept and welcome the Word of God which will take root in our hearts and save our souls.

Once we receive the Word of God in our hearts, we are to be action-oriented in doing His work. When we hear God's message, we are to do more than merely listen. We are not to deceive or betray ourselves and be satisfied as a hearer only which is contrary to God's truth. When we are a listener only without any action, we are like a person who looks in a mirror and then quickly forgets his own image.

God expects us to hear and heed His word and commands. We are to obey what He says and persevere in searching the scriptures to learn more about His will. Obedience to God brings His blessings. We may think we are more religious or righteous than others, but if we don't bridle our tongue, our outward works for God are futile and empty. Our actions for God are to be genuine and real.

James tells us plainly to look out after the legitimate needs of widows and orphans, and to be unspotted and uncontaminated from the world.

God blesses and allows us to profit from trials and temptations. We are to love Him when we come under fire from Satan. We cling to Him when the circumstances of life work against us. We are to let a thankful spirit be our guide instead of showing pride or self-pity. God expects us to be proactive in serving Him and our fellow-man. Love for God and love for our neighbor meet God's expectations.

Chapter Thirty-one
Faith and Works

The Christian has been ordered to do good works to demonstrate love for God and others. It is commendable to see people carry out this directive from the scriptures. Much good is accomplished when a helping hand is extended to someone with real needs they cannot meet. A neighbor may need help with firewood or fuel, or they may bring in a meal when someone is sick and immobile. There are so many ways we can help someone in need. A helping hand up is of great value to the receiver. The giver normally receives the greater blessing when they help someone who is truly in need.

Many agencies offer help on a much larger scale for families hit with strong storms or those who are trapped in a war-torn region. Many agencies can respond internationally to bring relief with food, clothes, medical services, and supplies. There are many legitimate faith-based charities whose mission is to meet people's physical and even their spiritual needs during their time of crisis. We have been instructed to also meet the needs of orphans and widows who don't have family support. Schools and orphanages dot the landscape of America as they house, feed, and educate orphans. This is an outreach opportunity for churches and individuals to prayerfully and financially support those who carry out God's command to love our fellow man.

<u>Impartiality</u>   (James 2:1-13)

Christians are responsible to treat everyone fairly and equally. It is not our privilege or place to prefer one person above another as God loves each of us the same. Normally our love is received by others with appreciation, but some reject love for whatever reason. In this case, we can pray on their behalf that the problem they currently have will be removed.

James says we are not to prefer the rich above the poor. A snobbish or selfish person is not doing God's will by preferential treatment of certain individuals or classes of people.

We are to follow Christ's example as he worked with the down-and-out, the diseased, and demon-possessed. Jesus did not have a problem dealing with saints or sinners. He pointed out people's sins and instructed them to clean up their lives, but it was up to each person to accept or reject what He said. Jesus worked with the Pharisees and religious leaders to show them a better way to worship God even though many of them rejected Him. He told idol worshipers to forsake their idols so they could follow God solely. Jesus was the same every day no matter who was in the audience.

Christians are warned in James 2:2-4 that we must be careful when a well-dressed person comes into our worship service, that we not pay more attention to them than someone less fortunate. It is easy for us to look on the outside of a person when God looks on the sincerity of every heart. James warns us to not discriminate and thereby become a judge or critic.

A perfect example of how God frowns on the proud and self-righteous person is found in Luke 18:10-14. Jesus spoke about a Pharisee who was one of the religious leaders and a tax collector who went to the temple to pray. The Pharisee thanked God that he was not like other men, and especially the tax collector. The religious person told God what a clean life he lived by fasting and giving tithes. The tax collector would not even lift his eyes toward heaven, but asked God to be merciful for he was a sinner. Jesus said the tax collector was justified by God. He stated further that whoever exalts himself will be humbled, and the humble person will be exalted before God.

God chose the poor in the eyes of the world to be rich in faith. If a person has accepted Christ as their Lord, they are near to God's heart. The faithful poor are promised an inheritance in God's kingdom. A person's value in God's sight cannot be determined by their physical net worth. A person can struggle every month to make ends meet for his family, but at the same time they are walking closely with God.

An illustration of this truth is found in a parable recorded in Luke 16:19-31. Jesus spoke about a very wealthy man and a destitute beggar. The rich man lived a life of luxury while the beggar whose name was Lazarus lay outside the rich man's gate each day. Lazarus only wanted the crumbs that fell from the rich man's table. Lazarus was covered with festering sores and the dogs would come and lick the sores. He needed food and medical relief, but the rich man ignored his needs.

Lazarus died and the angels carried him to Abraham's bosom in paradise. The rich man also died, was buried, and carried to Hades, the realm of the dead. The rich man was in torment and had become poor instantly when he died. His earthly wealth meant nothing in Hades. He looked a great distance from Hades into paradise and saw Lazarus who had instantly become rich and was being comforted.

Their roles reversed when they breathed their final breath on earth. The man in Hades called out to Abraham and asked for pity and mercy. He begged Abraham to send Lazarus to come and dip the tip of his finger in water to cool his tongue, for he was in anguish in the flaming fire. The rich man had just become a beggar. Abraham told the rich man to remember what he did during his life on earth. Abraham pointed out how he lived in ease and luxury while Lazarus had severe needs that he ignored.

Abraham told the rich man Lazarus was now comforted while he suffered in anguish. There was a great chasm between paradise and Hades and man cannot move from one place to the other once they are there.

Then the rich man begged Abraham to send Lazarus from paradise to his five brothers who were still alive on earth. Lazarus could warn his brothers to change so they would not land in Hades. Abraham said he would not send Lazarus to his brothers as they had Moses and the Prophets to hear and heed. The man thought if someone from the dead witnessed to his brothers they would surely listen and repent. He wanted his brothers to amend their ways and to hate their past sins.

Abraham told the man if his brothers would not listen to God's messengers from the past, they would not listen to Lazarus. Paradise and Hades are fixed by God and cannot be changed by man.

The rich man's previous possessions on earth did not make any difference to Abraham. Instead, he comforted Lazarus, the poor beggar. Our riches won't matter when we are on our death bed. Only our relationship with God, our families, and friends will matter.

James' letter was to the twelve tribes of Israel that were scattered throughout the known world. He told them in James 2:6-13 they had insulted and dishonored the poor. The rich had domineered over the children of Israel and hauled them into courts of law. The rich had slandered and blasphemed the Law that distinguished the children of Israel as God-fearing people. James commanded them to love their neighbor according to the scriptures.

He warned them if they continued to favor the rich, they would be convicted by their own Law as violators and offenders. James then makes a very strong statement. He said if they kept the whole Law and stumbled on one point, they had broken the entire Law. Their Law was very restrictive and judgmental. Christ came to fulfill the Law through His mercy and grace. James called this the law of liberty. James said if they had shown no mercy (*to the poor*), their judgment would be merciless; but mercy shown would result in victory.

<u>Faith without Works</u> (James 2:14-26)

James asked a pointed question in James 2:14: "What is the use (*profit*), my brethren, for anyone to profess to have faith if he has no (*good*) works (*to show for it*)?" We must be careful to distinguish between good works and God's plan of salvation. Good works are an outgrowth of our acceptance of Jesus who gives us salvation. Good works can never replace the need to repent of our sins, confess Christ as the Son of God, and be baptized into Him. James asked if such a faith without works can save his soul. Our faith in Christ and good works for our fellow-man go hand-in-hand.

If we see a person in need of food or clothing, we are expected to address their need. But, if we say, "May God bless you to meet your need," and don't offer help, James asked what good have we done? James is showing us the reality of being a Christian. We are to meet real needs, and not just offer soothing words, and then go on our way. Faith works the same way. Our faith triggers good deeds for others.

Faith requires works to become a working and active faith; otherwise, we only have a passive and inactive faith. Faith without good works is inoperative and dead. We show the world our faith by and through good works.

Christians believe in God the Father and His Son Jesus. The demons also believe in God and tremble. James asks the question if his hearers were willing to be shown *(proof)*, that faith apart from *(good)* works is inactive, ineffective, and worthless (James 2:20). He reminded them that their Father Abraham had a strong faith in God and he demonstrated his faith with good deeds throughout his lifetime. God tested Abraham's faith when He told him to take his only son, Isaac, to offer him on the mountain as a sacrifice and offering to Him.

Abraham obeyed God through faith and took Isaac to the mountain. After a three-day journey, Abraham bound Isaac and laid him on the altar. He drew his knife back to kill his son when an Angel of the Lord called out to him. The Angel told Abraham to not harm Isaac for He knew Abraham feared God and would not withhold anything from Him. Abraham had to show God his faith through his works. Abraham looked and saw a ram caught in a thicket that he could sacrifice to God.

Abraham completely believed and trusted in God. There was no doubt in his mind about God's love and faithfulness. He relied on God to meet his needs and spare his son. God saw Abraham's true faith and considered him a righteous man when he conformed to God's will.

We may never have a severe test of our faith like Abraham, but we must be just as willing to do whatever God says through the Holy Spirit and His Word. Our faith will surely be tested with the problems that come our way. Our faith is declared righteous when we conform to God's will. We are justified (*pronounced righteous before God*) through what we do with works of obedience in addition to what we believe.

Rahab was a harlot in the city of Jericho. Joshua 2:1-21 tells us Joshua sent two spies to Jericho to bring back information on their walls and troop strength. The spies lodged with Rahab while in Jericho. The king's men told him there were spies at Rahab's house. He sent word to her to send the men to him, for they were spies from Israel. Rahab wanted to protect the spies so she hid them on her roof. She told the king she didn't know they were spies and they had already left her house. Rahab sent word to the king the spies had gone through the gates of Jericho during the darkness and he should pursue and overtake them.

She then came to the roof where she had hidden the spies and told them all the people of Jericho feared Israel. They knew God was with Israel and its army.

The people of Jericho were aware how God had parted the Red Sea so the Israelites could escape the Egyptian army after being released from slavery. She told the spies the people of Jericho had lost courage to fight Israel because they knew God was with them. She asked them to show kindness and keep her family from dying when Israel would soon invade Jericho. They promised to protect Rahab's family when God gave Jericho to Israel. Rahab's house was built atop the outer wall of the city, so she lowered the spies that night with a rope through the window so they could escape.

It is interesting to note Rahab the harlot is mentioned in Hebrews 11:31, the Hall of Fame for other well-known people with a strong faith. Her faith in God and the spies Joshua sent saved her family from Israel's attack. She was justified and made right in the eyes of God for her faith and actions to save the spies. Her faith was active when she did good works and she was recognized for her protection for the spies.

James concludes his message on the value of faith and works by saying in James 2:26, "For as the human body apart from the spirit is lifeless, so faith apart from (*its*) works of obedience is also dead." Our body represents faith and our breath represents our works. The body is dead without breath just as faith is dead without works.

Chapter Thirty-two
The Tongue and Wisdom

The book of James gives some practical guidance to every Christian. We need to know what God expects so we can live according to His will. So far, James has addressed profit through trials, the mistake of showing favoritism for certain individuals, loving God during trials, Christian attributes needed to get through trials with victory, having an active faith, and the necessity of faith that produces good works. Now James takes us a little further down this journey by showing the damage of a tongue that is out of control. James then shows the difference between heavenly versus demonic wisdom.

Navigating the Christian life is not always simple or easy. We are faced with many decisions on problems that crop up with no forewarning. We use our own logic and good judgment, but also call on God for guidance from the Holy Spirit. There is always an answer to every problem, but we may not necessarily like the answer. God promises to answer our prayers if we pray according to His will, but we may not like His response or His response time. God always acts according to His will and on His timetable.

Jesus went to the garden to pray on the night of His betrayal. He agonized in prayer with God three times. He was under so much stress His sweat became as great drops of blood (Luke 22:44). After praying twice that night, He finally relented in His third prayer and accepted God's will to go to the cross to die for our sins. There was no reason for Him to die in our place, except it was God's will. God did not deliver Him from the cross even though Jesus pleaded for deliverance initially.

It takes a strong faith to pray for God's will to be done in our life. If we don't know His will, it is unnerving to surrender our self to God and seek His will. We don't know the price we will pay for total submission to God.

Through faith, we know God works all things out for our eventual good, but we can be fearful of what we may face when He takes full charge of our life. This is where faith and trust come into play. It is natural to fear the unknown, even the unknown will of God. When we surrender fully to God, we can count on His provision and blessings.

The Tongue (James 3:1-12

Our tongues can speak blessings or curses. We can use our tongues for good or evil. Negotiators bargain at the peace table as they try and find a solution to a raging conflict. Married couples try to verbally work out family issues within the marriage or with their children. God gave us our tongues for good reason, so we need to use good reason when we speak.

James said not many people should become teachers (*in church*) due to the heavy responsibility of trying to train others. Teaching takes self-discipline and forethought. Diligent teachers are concerned that they do not create problems or division. Teachers in the church will be judged by a higher standard because of their leadership position of trying to influence others on spiritual matters. We must lead and teach by example so others will be inclined to heed what we say and follow our footsteps.

Every person, including teachers, is apt to stumble and fall on their Christian journey. It is so easy to say something that may cause division and confusion. A caring teacher feels a responsibility to never offend as they teach. Sometimes the truth offends, but it is the teacher's responsibility to hold to the facts even if it does offend. He/she must strive to live a blameless life and be strong enough to control their daily actions.

Farmers and equestrians put bits in their horse's mouths so they can control the horse to gee or haw to the right or the left when they tighten either rein. The bit is small and the horse is large, but the bit controls the whole horse.

Likewise, the small rudder on a huge ship keeps it on course or turns the ship to correct its direction. The helmsman in the wheel house determines when to steer right or left to turn the huge vessel. The tongue is small like the bit or a rudder, but it can quickly change the course of our life for good or bad. The tongue can start a verbal fire or it can be a peacemaker. It can contaminate and deprave our life and set fire to the lives of others. It can destroy a lifetime relationship with a few misspoken words. Beasts and birds can be tamed by man, but we cannot tame someone else's tongue. It can be restless and undisciplined, full of evil and poison.

With the tongue, we bless God or curse man who is made in God's image. A fountain cannot issue both fresh and salt water but the tongue is different. It can damage or bring healing at our discretion. Every person is accountable to God for how they use their tongue. A fig tree or a grapevine can only produce its own intended fruit. A child of God bears fruit that pleases Him and hopefully encourages our fellow man.

A tongue that is under control belongs to a person with godly wisdom, who is filled with humble service. Speak words of encouragement instead of judgment. Let your words be based on truth and not lies. Our tongues should build up, not tear others down.

<u>Heavenly and Demonic Wisdom</u>   (James 3:13-18)

James asks, "Who is there among you who are wise and intelligent?" True wisdom comes from a person who lives honorably, has humility, and does good works. A wise and intelligent person is not a braggart or selfish individual.

Their eyes and ears are open to use their God-given talents and resources to aid others who have legitimate needs. Our first financial obligation is to God who expects the tithe to be brought into His storehouse, the church. Then we are to look for opportunities to help others around us.

James changes direction in his discourse when he said a person who espouses envy, jealousy, and selfishness cannot take pride while they are in defiance to the Truth of God's Word. Godly people do not argue with the Bible. A selfish stance creates confusion and disunity that incubate evil and vile practices.

We seek to replace bitterness and jealousy with a sweet spirit and acceptance of the other person's success. There should be celebration or weeping for our neighbor's success or loss. We take God's Word at face value without trying to alter its meaning. We are not in God's will when we try to bend His word to suit our lifestyle. James calls this superficial wisdom that is not from God. Satan promotes earthly superficial wisdom that downgrades God's Word. When we have difficulty applying God's Word to our lives, it is time to ask for His help to transform our lives to be in compliance to His will.

God's wisdom for man promotes a pure and undefiled attitude. Our lives are to be open books for God and man to see. The common person without much education can be just as powerful a witness for the Lord as the man who has graduated from seminary. The way we live and act is a strong message for others to observe and follow. People look beyond our credentials and possessions to the way our lives are lived. A pure life becomes the sermon we preach. We yield to reason and are filled with compassion and good fruits. Wisdom from God is impartial and free from doubts and wavering. God's wisdom and the Bible are like a compass that keeps the ship (*our spiritual lives*) on course.

In Matthew 5, Jesus taught His disciples the Beatitudes. These are blessings we find when we practice the precepts of God. Jesus talked about the poor in spirit, mourners, the meek, those who hunger and thirst after righteousness, the merciful, the pure in heart, and the persecuted. He said we can be blessed and find happiness in all these circumstances. In Matthew 5:9, Jesus said, "Blessed (*happy*) are the peacemakers, for they shall be called the sons of God!" We are to both make and maintain peace with God and our neighbor. God smiles on us when we seek peace for His sake.

If we want to be a productive fruit-bearer for God, we must strive to make peace. There will be a harvest sent from God when we conform to His will in thought and deed. This harvest comes from seed that is sown in peace by peace-lovers. The results of the harvest include agreement and harmony between individuals. When there is peace, our minds are free from conflicts and fears. Individuals, churches, and nations all need fewer troublemakers and more peacemakers who can bring harmony and unity in times of disagreement. We can thank Satan for conflicts, division, and disagreement for these come from seeds of evil. The good seed of God will produce unity and agreement.

Unity

We look beyond James' teaching to other scriptures about unity. Peacemakers are motivated by a strong desire for unity instead of strife. Unity can overcome strife when our minds and attitudes are ripe for a positive change.

The first step to being a peacemaker and promoting unity is to be united with Christ. We are united with Him when we accept Him as our Savior.

We confess Him as the Son of God so we can become a child of God, and a joint heir with Christ to all God's riches. Our relationship with Christ is likened to a marriage. We love and adore Him and accept Him as our spiritual life partner as our loyalty is to Christ above all others.

A couple of references to being one in Christ are mentioned in 1 Corinthians 10. Paul referred to the time when the Jews' ancestors were in the wilderness for 40 years after their release from slavery in Egypt. They all ate the same manna God sent every day and drank from the same spiritual Rock (*Christ*) who followed them.

We are also united with Christ when we observe the Lord's Supper. Jesus asked His disciples in 1 Corinthians 10:16-17, "The cup of blessing (*wine*) upon which we ask (*God's*) blessing, does it not mean (*that in drinking of it*) we participate in and share a fellowship in the body of Christ? The bread which we break, does it not mean (*that in eating it*) we participate in and share a fellowship (*communion*) in the body of Christ? For we are one body, because we all partake of the one Bread." Coming around the Lord's Table was never intended as a ritual of worship, but a time to re-connect with Christ. Jesus said in 1 Corinthians 11:25b-26, "Do this, as often as you drink (*it*), to call me (*affectionately*) to remembrance. For every time you eat this bread and drink this cup, you are representing and signifying and proclaiming the fact of the Lord's death until He comes."

When we come to His Table, we come to remember His sacrifice for us on the cross. The observance of the Lord's Supper will continue until He comes back. We need to remember Christ's sacrifice and come to His Table often as we celebrate His death and resurrection.

The Holy Spirit dwells in our hearts after we are baptized. The Holy Spirit is our daily Helper and Comforter.

Paul said in Philippians 1:27, "Only be sure as citizens so to conduct yourselves (*that*) your manner of life (*will be*) worthy of the good news (*the Gospel*) of Christ, so that whether I come and see you or am absent, I may hear this of you: that you are standing firm in united spirit and purpose, striving side by side, and contending with a single mind for the faith of the glad tidings (*the Gospel*)." We need the help of the Holy Spirit to bind believers together in unity, for we are all one in Christ. We must have unity to carry the banner of Christ into the world, just as an army moves forward as one unit.

Peter's prayer in 1 Peter 3:8 was, "Finally, all (*of you*) should be of one and the same mind (*united in spirit*), sympathizing (*with one another*), loving (*each other*) as brethren (*of one household*), compassionate and courteous (*tenderhearted and humble*)." Humility, compassion, and sympathy are the seeds we sow when we are united in Christ. Families, the church, and the world all need unity. We strive for and find unity in Christ.

Chapter Thirty-three
Pride and Boasting

James was led by the Holy Spirit to write things we might not like to read, but these things are what help us grow in Christ. James gives us the positive and the negative to strengthen our faith and fully surrender our lives to Christ. He shows us the difference between the seeds of good and the seeds of evil. We must keep our spiritual house uncluttered from the things of Satan so we can thrive as a child of God.

James addresses the obvious problems that come from pride and boasting. A proud person is a polar opposite of a humble person. Proverbs 3:34 and 1 Peter 5.5b say, "For God sets Himself against the proud (*overbearing, boastful*) – (*and He opposes*), but gives grace (*favor*) to the humble." This sums up in a nutshell what God thinks of a proud and boastful person who thinks they are better than everyone else. A person can be overly proud of their education, accomplishments, and achievements. God is the source of all our blessings whether they are great or small. We need to humbly thank and give Him glory for all we have.

Pride Produces Strife (James 4:1-6)

James opens with two questions in James 4:1, "What leads to strife (*discord and feuds*) and secondly, how do conflicts (*quarrels*) originate? Do they not arise from sensual desires that are ever warring in our bodily members?" Sin and selfishness lead to disunity and disagreement. We want our way no matter who it hurts. When this is our attitude, Satan is in control of our thoughts and actions. The other person's desires mean little as we are bound to have our way.

We may have problems of jealousy and covetousness (*wanting what others have*) but our desires go unfulfilled. When this happens, other bad things are probably going to follow.

James says we can even become a murderer as a result of pride getting its way. To hate someone is the same as murder, even if we don't use a weapon. Our envy and anger can rage within when we don't get our way. We want something and we want it now (*instant gratification*). In our weakened spiritual strength, we may allow Satan to lead us to do ungodly things against our friend or neighbor. There is no place for pride or selfishness with the child of God. We must look beyond self and at the bigger picture if the Holy Spirit is to lead us where God wants us to go.

We ask God for our needs, and if our lives are righteous and we pray within God's will, He has promised to answer. Sometimes we don't have because we don't ask God (1 John 3:15). We must ask with the right purpose and motive that will benefit the kingdom of God and also meet our needs. It is easy to pray selfishly with the wrong motive in mind. We can use God's blessings for selfish purposes if we aren't careful.

The miracles Jesus humbly performed were done to bring glory to God for His power and provision. Jesus wanted the people to see God working through Him. This should also be our objective.

In our cross-bearing for Christ, we must nail selfishness, pride, and ego to the cross. These things must be surrendered to God if we want His full and rich blessings. He can bless us abundantly and beyond our expectations when we serve Him fully. We serve without hesitation or doubt that He will supply all our needs.

When we accept Christ, we become one of His. The church (*believers*) is the bride of Christ, so our relationship with Him is for a lifetime.

When we pray with the wrong motive, we are living like a wayward and unfaithful spouse. We have love affairs with the world like a spouse who is unfaithful to their mate. Being a friend to the world means we are an enemy of God. We have forsaken our relationship with Christ to be loyal to Satan. We have taken an open stand against God (James 4:4). The Old Testament prophet Jeremiah spoke of unfaithful children of God and he told them to return to God. God said, "I am Lord and Master and Husband to you." (Jeremiah 3:14) God takes our marriage relationship with Christ seriously, and so should we. There is no room in the relationship for unfaithfulness or infidelity, just as in an earthly marriage.

James echoes this thought in James 4:5 where he talks about God's jealous love for us. We must yearn for the Spirit of God to dwell in our hearts as we strive to live faithfully. We want our love relationship with Christ to last until we breathe our final breath.

Pride and selfishness are evil. God sets Himself against the proud and haughty but gives grace to the lowly and humble (James 4:6). The humble are able to receive God's grace. He gives more and more grace to help us deal with our evil tendencies. We don't deserve His favor, but He gives it, nevertheless. He resists the proud while giving grace to the humble.

The Cure of Humility (James 4:7-10)

Humility and our love for Christ is the cure for the evil in our world. Many evil actions are taken for selfish reasons. Sometimes when a massacre occurs, there is no clear-cut reason for the shooter to do his evil deed. While murders are at epidemic proportions, there are many other evil acts happening every day. Satan is on the loose and it seems he is out of control, but one day God will rein him in and cast him into a lake of fire where he will spend eternity. Selfishness is an inward sin while humility is an outward blessing to honor God and benefit others.

We are subjects of God so we must resist the devil. We are promised in James 4:7 when we resist the devil and take a firm stand against him, he will flee from us. When he knows we are a Christian and our allegiance is to Christ, he backs off, at least for the moment. That does not mean our temptations to sin are gone forever. We live in the flesh and our bodies are naturally subject to sin. Satan will keep coming back to tempt us and draw us away from God. Let Satan know you are a child of God and you want no part of his lies and deceit.

As we meditate on the Word of God and open our hearts to the Holy Spirit, He draws us closer. God will draw closer to us as we seek Him diligently. We come to God as sinners who have been saved through His grace. Jesus' blood washes away our sins as He is our sacrificial Lamb. We may have drifted from God and committed spiritual adultery, but He stands ready for us to come back. God is willing to grant second chances, so we should never refuse to swallow our pride or say we are unworthy to come back to Him. We are unworthy in our eyes, but not in God's.

We come back to God in repentance for our sins. Our disloyalty may cause us to grieve and even weep because we have violated our relationship with Him. It is natural to feel remorse for our sins, but God can and will lift us back up on our spiritual feet when we let Him know we want to restore the relationship with Him. In humility, we come feeling insignificant in God's presence. He will exalt us and make our lives significant and meaningful once again.

<u>Judging</u> (James 4:11-12)
We break God's Law and His commandment when we speak evil against someone. When we criticize our brother, we are criticizing God's Law of love.

We judge the Law when we judge another person. James makes it very clear in James 4:12 that there is only one Judge and Lawgiver, and that is God. He does not give us the privilege or responsibility to be anyone's judge. We should thank God that we are not to judge. We would judge a person based on human standards, but God judges based on His higher standards including mercy and pardon. Human judgment can be unjust, but God's judgment will be just and deserved. God is able to both judge and destroy and He holds absolute power over life and death. We should never personally assume the position of judging as this is a clear violation of God's plan.

We might judge based on assumptions, but God's judgment will be based solely on the truth and facts. This should motivate each of us to draw as close to God as possible so we can face His judgment with confidence. We know He is a fair and righteous Judge, and this should enable us to approach His throne of judgment with a reverential fear of being in His presence. We serve an awesome and loving God.

<u>The Hope of Tomorrow</u> (James 4:13-17)
There is a natural tendency for us to say what we are going to do tomorrow or in the future. Perhaps we have made plans for weeks or

months for a future trip or activity. We plan even though life is fragile and uncertain. We may plan while putting the uncertainty of the future in the back of our mind. In reality, we don't know if we will live to see tomorrow. Perhaps Christ will come back today or tonight. Humans have zero control over tomorrow until it arrives.

James tells us in James 4:14 that we don't know in the least what tomorrow holds. Our lives are compared to a wisp of vapor, a puff of smoke, or a mist. Vapors, smoke, and mists appear for a very short while and they are gone.

They disappear into thin air as if they never existed. Our earthly life is the same way, but the good news is our heavenly life will last for eternity. James tells us to say if only the Lord is willing we will carry out our future plans. God holds us in the palm of His hand and only He knows how many days or years we will have on earth. We boast falsely when we presume we will have a tomorrow. All boasting is wrong in God's eyes.

The rich farmer in Jesus' parable that we mentioned in an earlier chapter assumed he would have a tomorrow as he planned to tear down his barns and build larger ones to hold his abundant crop. God called the farmer a fool for planning without asking for God's guidance. It is very easy for us to get in front of God when we start making plans on our own. He holds the future while we only have the present moment. We aren't even promised the rest of today, much less tomorrow. This is not being morbid for it is God's fact.

King Solomon confirmed the brevity and uncertainty of time when he said in Proverbs 27:1, "Do not boast of tomorrow, for you know not what a day may bring forth." Time is uncertain for the young and old, the healthy and ill.

The Old Testament prophet said in Isaiah 57:1, "The righteous man perishes, and no one lays it to heart; and merciful and devout men are taken away, with no one considering that the uncompromisingly upright and godly person is taken away from the calamity and evil to come." When a younger person dies, we may question God on why the person left so soon. God sees the long-term picture while we only see the past. God may have spared a loved one by taking them early in their life so He could spare them from some tragic future problem had they lived.

Christians sometimes struggle with Romans 8:28 that says, "We are assured and know that all things work together and are for good to and for those who love God and are called according to (*His*) design and purpose."

When we experience a loss through death or a broken relationship and don't understand why, we have this verse that tells us God has a plan that works for our good in all cases. Admittedly, it takes a strong faith to accept this verse at face value when we suffer a severe loss, but through faith we must.

In summary, conquer your pride and strive for humility. A humble person is a blessing to God and others. Don't fall into Satan's trap when tempted to judge someone as God relieved us of this responsibility. Live your best one day at a time, for this is all we are promised on this earth. We hope God will bless us with long life, but that is totally in His hands. Our challenge is to live every day as if it is our last day on earth. We are assured of His love and concern, so He always acts in our best interest, even when we don't understand His timing or plan.

Chapter Thirty-four
Perseverance

Enduring to the end of a strenuous activity takes patience and commitment. A runner whose lungs seem to be on fire during the race must fight through pain if he/she will reach the finish line. All athletes know firsthand what it is to play through pain. Some projects in medicine or business may take years to fully execute but the project managers or researchers keep the goal of a successful completion visible so they can finish their long-term task. When we are in the midst of a difficult task, we may feel bogged down with no end in sight. If we keep chipping away at the task, we soon see the finish line in sight. This motivates us to buckle down for the final sprint.

A Christian is very much like an athlete since we have a definitive goal in mind. We can't see the finish line yet, but we know eternity awaits. Our Christian walk has mountains, valleys, smooth, and rough spots. When we are mired in a problem, we need to determine if it is a game changer for life or if we are dealing with a bend in the road. This helps us put our problem in perspective so we can endure to the end.

Our prize at the end of an earthly project may be a physical reward, a completed remodeling project on our house, or a spiritual reward. When we strive for our reward, we find the motivation and energy to keep moving forward.

James 5 is broken down into four segments: 1) the fate of the rich, 2) patience in persevering, 3) meeting specific needs and 4) bringing back an erring believer.

<u>The Fate of the Rich</u> (James 5:1-6)

There is nothing sinful about being rich. King David, his son King Solomon, and Job were all very rich men in the Old Testament and all three men were God-fearing. Their riches did not deter them from a personal relationship with God.

God gave King David the specifications to build an elaborate temple in Jerusalem. David gathered domestic and imported building materials such as cedar lumber, precious gems, metals, tapestries, etc. to erect and adorn the new temple. This would be God's house and a place where the children of Israel would be proud to come and worship. God told David before construction began to finish putting all the materials in storage so his son Solomon could actually build the temple. God wanted every detail in His specifications met.

Solomon turned out to be a very wealthy ruler during his reign as king.

Job was a wealthy farmer and rancher. He had ten children and thousands of heads of livestock. He automatically had to have farming equipment and storage facilities to hold the crops so he could feed his animals and meet his family's needs. Job lost all his children and possessions in a strong windstorm one day, but due to his persistent faith, God restored all his animals and other assets. He also had more children to replace those he tragically lost. He persevered in his faith and God rewarded him accordingly.

Wealthy people must oversee and manage their assets; otherwise, they can lose a fortune in a short period of time. James talks about the wealthy unfavorably in the fifth chapter of his book. He tells them to weep and lament over the miseries and woes that will surely come upon them. Their abundant wealth had rotted and ruined and their beautiful garments were moth-eaten.

Their gold and silver was completely rusted through and corroded. The rust was a testimony against the wealthy. Their wealth would devour their flesh as if it were afire. Through devious means, they had accumulated much wealth and treasures for their last days.

This is a terrible pronouncement on the rich, but what is the meaning? James is rebuking them for their arrogance and selfishness toward others. They had not shared with the less fortunate as they continued piling up more and more. A rich person may not have a specific goal in mind on how much wealth they need to reach a satisfaction point; they know they just want more. One of the problems with riches is that we can place our dependence on them and make them an idol. This blocks our allegiance to God who blessed us with what we have. The rich can easily take the position of an owner instead of being God's steward of his estate.

The rich had withheld wages their workers had earned. They had defrauded their field help who brought their bountiful harvest into the barns. Workers were normally paid each day at the end of the shift and they knew what it was to live hand-to-mouth. The workers complained because they had been short-changed on money they had rightfully earned, but their cries fell on the deaf ears of the rich but God heard the cries of the abused workers.

The rich had turned to a soft and luxurious lifestyle and experienced the pleasures of self-indulgence and self-gratification. They fattened their hearts, but the day of reckoning was coming when justice would be done. They fattened themselves like a cow that would soon be slaughtered. They had even murdered innocent men who offered no resistance. The abusive rich people were facing judgment with blood on their hands and treasures that meant nothing to God.

<u>Patience through Persevering</u>   (James 5:7-12)

James now directs our attention to the coming of the Lord. We must practice patience until Christ comes and takes care of all injustices. The farmer knows about patience as he awaits the upcoming harvest from his fields. He tilled, planted, fed, and weeded but now he must patiently await the rain and the harvest. All his hard labor is in the ground waiting on God to give a bountiful harvest.

Christians must also patiently wait on the coming of Christ. Our faith must be steadfast without doubting as the scriptures tell us His coming is near. We accept this truth in faith believing every word of His promise. Waiting is very difficult. We get impatient while a loved one is in surgery or undergoing a treatment. We pray for God to make them well and whole again. Waiting on the coming of the Lord is something we want to happen sooner rather than later. We learn patience in the school of hard knocks.

Psalms 33:20 says, "Our inner selves wait *(earnestly)* for the Lord; He is our Help and our Shield." We eagerly look for the Lord's coming. This takes patience, but God gives us strength to endure to the end. Jeremiah the prophet tells us in Lamentations 3:25, "The Lord is good to those who wait hopefully and expectantly for Him, to those who seek Him and require Him *(by right of necessity and on the authority of God's word)*." Our patience will be rewarded when we breathe our final breath and leave this world to dwell with Him. We earnestly and eagerly look for His coming to rapture the church.

James 5:9 teaches us to not complain against one another as the Judge is standing at the door. We know He is coming; we just don't know when. We are to accept the promise of His coming as told by the Old Testament prophets and the New Testament scriptures. We are to follow the example of the Old Testament prophets as they waited patiently on the Messiah to be born. We now patiently and eagerly look for His coming back to rapture His church. What a resurrection day that will be.

James once again directs our attention to Job, the rich farmer and rancher who lost it all.

We are to look at Job's endurance and his steadfast faith that did not waiver during his darkest days. God richly blessed Job in the end. He lost everything, but God restored it all. Jesus looks on us today in pity and compassion just as God viewed Job. He loves us in tenderness and mercy. We may be suffering unduly but be assured God loves you with His everlasting love that never fades away. He can restore all our losses when we trust in Him.

James admonishes us to keep our mouths free from profanity or to not take an oath. Our word should be the only bond we need for people to place their confidence in us. There are a few exceptions that come to mind. When a person is sworn into public office they are asked to take an oath to uphold the Constitution. When witnesses testify in a court of law, they are asked to take an oath that they will tell the truth. We should never take God's name in vain when talking with others.

Meeting Serious Needs (James 5:13-18)

James 5:13-15 gives anyone who is fighting evil some very specific instructions. If we are fighting Satan, we should pray and if we have just won a victory over Satan, we should sing and praise God. If anyone is sick, he/she should call the elders of the church to anoint them with oil in the name of the Lord and pray for them (James 5:14). We are promised healing and restoration if we have sought forgiveness of our sins. Sometimes God answers our prayers quickly, but if it is not His will to heal a person in this life, He will surely heal them when they arrive in paradise.

We are told to confess our faults to each other. All of us have taken false steps or uttered words we wish we could recall. We are encouraged to pray for one another to receive healing and restoration of a broken relationship. We are promised an earnest prayer from a righteous person makes dynamic and tremendous power available from God.

If we err in our walk of faith, our brother is directed to bring us back to the truth and to God. Whoever turns a sinner from his evil course will save that person's soul from the second death. His/her sins will receive pardon from Christ.

James was a late believer in Jesus as the Son of God, but he offers all who will listen guidance on how to live honorably before God. He told us in the book of James the good and the bad since life is not always pleasant. Our walk with God is filled with blessings, but we must always be on the alert for Satan's deception to try and lead us away from God. The success of our daily walk with God depends largely on our devotion to studying His Word and staying in close communication with Him in our prayer life. As we study and pray, the Holy Spirit is present to show us the path of righteousness that is pleasing to God.

God's love for every person is amazing. We may shun or reject Him, but He still loves us with His everlasting love. He patiently waits on us to come to Him in complete faith that our salvation is found in Jesus, His Son.

One day we will pass from this life if Jesus does not come back first. If we have accepted Christ, our souls will go to be with the Lord and our bodies will be laid to rest. Jesus will come back to rapture His church when God says it is time and He will bring the saints with Him. Our bodies that have been asleep in Jesus will come forth from the grave and we will rise to meet the Lord in the air.

We eagerly await His return when we will be with God for all eternity. Today is the day of salvation, so our prayer is for those who have not accepted Christ as Lord. May today be the day you accept Jesus as your Lord so you, too, can stand on the promises of God.

About the Author

Don was born at home in Tazewell County, Virginia. His dad was a coal miner and his mother worked hard to raise five children. Our parents had a strong work ethic matched by a tenacious faith in God. Even though resources were limited, our family was rich in love for the Lord and each other.

Don went to business school after graduating from high school. He worked his way through a maze of different jobs from entry level to management. His jobs ranged from administrative positions to vice president of a furniture manufacturer. Then he went into field sales calling on the military and universities. He was blessed as many doors closed, but just as many better ones were opened by the Lord.

Don has always been blessed to be fully involved in the Lord's work. For many years, he worked in the areas of music, administration, and teaching the Bible. In October 2014, his elders asked him to become the minister of his church and he still holds this position.

His family has gone through several deaths just as others have experienced, but God continues to bless. We have the blessed hope of Jesus' return to earth when families will be re-united and we will forever be with the Lord. We eagerly await His return when all things will be made new.

www.ingramcontent.com/pod-product-compliance
Lightning Source LLC
Chambersburg PA
CBHW071236160426
43196CB00009B/1086